Notes on Womanhood

T0158756

KA HAEA TE ATA
KA HAEA TE ATA

NOTES ON

Womanhood

A conversation about gender and identity

Sarah Jane Barnett

OTAGO UNIVERSITY PRESS
Te Whare Tā o Te Wānanga o Ōtākou
otago.ac.nz/press

'I entered adulthood as two people: the image my era wanted me to be, and the other woman, the hidden one, the one with a body.'

— Eve Fairbanks

'I have no idea what to call this rebirth
and yet I'm here to name it
to feed the new flame ...'

— Hinemoana Baker

For Sheila and Pauline and Nikki

Contents

Chapter One
Women without a uterus

My mother used to wear a purple suit. It had a single button on the boxy jacket that pulled it in at her waist. The skirt was tight and smooth. The first time I remember her wearing the suit was at my cousin's wedding, a lavish church affair in Ōtepoti Dunedin where the bride and groom arrived at the reception by helicopter. But she would also wear it on normal work days. My mum's friends – we'd bump into them at the local mall or in the aisles of the supermarket, my sister and I hanging off her arm – would come up to her, and after making polite conversation say, 'You look so good, Pauline.' They'd stand back a bit, cast an eye over her suited body and say, 'Have you lost some weight?'

My mother's a renowned public health academic and has always been an outspoken feminist. I remember one time during high school when she was driving my friend and me into central Ōtautahi Christchurch to go to the movies. He made some sexist joke about a woman's place being in the kitchen. Mum pulled the car over and in a steely tone told my friend to get out. I remember feeling stunned but impressed. When I was born, my mother only had three months' maternity leave. After that ended, she would bathe and feed me in the early morning, go to work, come home and feed me again at lunchtime before going all the way back in to work. When my sister and I were school-aged, my mother worked for a university medical school during the day while she wrote her PhD at night.

One school holiday, all of us crammed into a motel room in a Te Waipounamu South Island town, my father told my mother that she was too fat for him to love her any more. I remember spittle at the corner of my father's mouth and the anguish on my mother's face. I remember staring hard at the squiggly-green-patterned wallpaper of the room. I wasn't able to sleep till late that night, my sad little body deep in the bed.

Those motels always had a pool that the kids (my younger sister and I took the other guests as our immediate best friends) would splash in and out of all day. We would spread out our towels beside the pool and bake in our neon swimsuits. Somewhere in the motel grounds there would be a rusted swing set and a television room where the adults could socialise and drink shandies. I loved these holidays, even with the strain between my parents. They were good people in a hard situation that, as a kid, I couldn't understand. What I did understand was that a few months after the holiday my mother had lost weight and bought a purple suit. That people liked her better that way. That *she* was better.

I've been thinking about womanhood – about what it means to me, and what I've been taught – since I had a hysterectomy a few years back. Twelve years earlier I'd had surgery to remove precancerous cells from my cervix. I knew that if the cells returned I might need surgery again, but I never expected a hysterectomy.

The gynaecologist gave me the news as we sat in his spacious office, light streaming in through the large windows. The air punched into my chest as he told me I needed to have my uterus and fallopian tubes removed. They'd found some new abnormal cells on my cervix. This type of cancer produced 'skip lesions', he said. There could be abnormal cells and then healthy ones, but then other abnormal cells could be hidden elsewhere. If he simply took out the abnormal cervical cells he couldn't guarantee they hadn't skipped to my uterus. An image came to me of standing on the pebbly bank of a river and teaching my son, Sam, how to skip a stone. Of how lightly the flat grey mass skimmed across the water. I was forty. I didn't want any more children, so full removal was the best option. He would also have a look at my ovaries during the surgery to see if they needed to come out too.

I felt numb. The gynaecologist was sitting at his desk with official-looking papers spread before him. I was in a low squishy armchair and he felt high above me. His legs were spread apart, one elbow rested on each knee as he told me the news. He cracked a few jokes as he talked. He was wearing a grey suit with a white shirt casually unbuttoned.

At the end of the appointment he printed out a stack of medical literature for me to read. 'These are written for doctors, so let me know if you have trouble,' he said. He leaned forward and said, 'Don't worry, the operation won't make you less of a woman.'

I think most women will recognise this moment – a man who wants to be kind but who has few narratives to work with: the male saviour; the expert. It's my experience that this man does not do well when confronted with a self-possessed woman. Sitting in his office I told him that I was more than competent to read the literature, and that I was fully aware of what made up my womanhood. Confusion flickered across his face and he laughed a little. He smoothed his suit jacket and then continued to reassure me.

In her celebrated blog on why saggy boobs matter, Chidera Eggerue writes, 'There is literally no wrong way to be a woman. There is literally no wrong way to have a body as long as your body is functioning well enough to keep you alive.'[1] As a child, I was always the first to dive into a cold swimming pool, the water a shock on my skin. I'd hold my breath, swim down and place my toes on the blue-tiled bottom, my body pure joy in the silence. That day, I wish I'd told the gynaecologist that to school me on womanhood was to take something that was not his. I wish I'd climbed into bed with my mum that night years ago at the motel and told her she was loved.

/

A month after I saw the gynaecologist, my husband Jim dropped me at a hospital in Te Whanganui-a-Tara Wellington, the city where we live. I followed a nurse as she led me down the long corridors to my room. A single bed and a comfortable armchair. Fluorescent lighting and beige walls. A small en suite. A private hospital room. She bustled around as I stripped behind a curtain and pulled on a blue hospital gown. She had me produce a urine sample, gave me the dinner menu and left me sitting on the bed.

Jim and I couldn't afford to pay for me to have the operation privately. We barely had enough leave to take time off for my recovery, let alone savings to pay for private surgery. But my parents had called a few days after the news about the hysterectomy and offered to pay. They gave me some good reasons why they should: it would mean the surgery could be done sooner; they hoped private would mean better results and a faster recovery; this sort of thing is what their savings were for. They knew I was scared and didn't want me to suffer the anxiety of long public hospital waiting lists. They wanted me to be safe and well. I felt lightheaded at how much the operation was costing my parents. I felt ashamed and undeserving to have the choice. But mostly I felt grateful.

Waiting in the hospital room I read *Tomboy Survival Guide* by Ivan Coyote, a collection of short stories about Coyote growing up butch in Canada in the 1970s. I'd seen Coyote speak at a writers' festival some years before and had brushed away tears in a dark auditorium as I listened to them speak about love and gender. The first story in *Tomboy Survival Guide*, 'Not My Son', is about Coyote, who was assigned female at birth, being mistaken for a boy as a child. In this story Coyote describes how they started to intentionally present as a boy, but is quick to say, 'I didn't not want to be a girl because I had been told that they were weaker or somehow lesser than boys ... I just always knew that I wasn't.'[2]

If anything, the women in Coyote's family were seen as stronger than the men because they 'handled most of the practical details of everyday life.'[3] That echoes my experience of growing up in the 1980s and 90s: many women, including my own mum, were in charge of the household, the children, the finances and the social relationships. The difference: women were now also working. The slogan for the early 90s was the well-meaning 'Girls can do anything', which Mum cheerfully repeated to me from our newly renovated kitchen, an apron tied over her work clothes while she cooked the evening meal. I think we even had a magnet with the slogan on our fridge. My mother as worker ant – she carried giant leaves and twigs, fifty times her weight.

In Eve Fairbanks' article '"We believed we could remake ourselves any way we liked": how the 1990s shaped #MeToo', she writes that to understand how women feel today we must understand the 90s – 'a peculiar era, caught between the confidence that there had been fabulous progress in the relationship between the sexes, and the smouldering remnants of a past in which bold women were feared and ridiculed.'[4]

Fairbanks describes the intense pressure felt by women in the 90s. Suddenly everything was possible. She points to *The Powerpuff Girls*, *Sweet Valley High* and 'fuck-me boots' (mine were black leather with a blocky heel and a zip up the side) as 90s narratives of female empowerment and ambition, albeit not without contradiction.[5] *Sweet Valley High*'s twins, Jessica the manipulative party girl and Elizabeth the sensible and studious nerd, were a modern version of the Madonna/whore dichotomy. Or as Fairbanks says of Princess Diana, '[she] was applauded for rejecting her ugly prince. But she was also painted as reckless for getting killed with her playboy lover in a car chase with paparazzi.'[6]

And I can't forget the Spice Girls – the Madonna/whore stereotypes expanded into Baby, Sporty, Ginger, Posh and Scary: five personas that are equally reductive while simultaneously advertising themselves as 'girl power'. I was a Spice Girls fan as a teenager, singing along to '2 Become 1' and 'Wannabe' in my bedroom, but I could never settle on which Spice was my favourite – I knew I was a bit like all of them. 'To acknowledge how younger women have struggled,' Fairbanks goes on to say, 'would entail a painful admission that the battles of previous generations may not have been won as decisively as they had hoped.'[7]

I thought about this while reading Coyote in the hospital room. While the slogan my mother told me was 'Girls can do anything', what I heard and took right into my bones was 'Women must do everything'. Feminist Jessica Eaton says, 'For women to be valid, whole human beings in society – feminism has got to move beyond this notion that women are striving for what men already have.'[8] The problem with the 90s was that women were not able to create something new: they were given some of what men had while being expected to continue the traditional work and roles of women. The space had not yet opened – and still may not have – for women to rise from the ashes of their old selves. Mum's cheerfulness at the time was actually hidden defiance. When I asked her about it years later she said, 'I wouldn't let the bastards win.'

Eventually the nurse came back. I'd talked to the anaesthetist and now it was time for surgery. She had me lie down on the bed under the covers. I tucked my arms in close to my side and lay there stiff and terrified. She flicked off the brakes and wheeled me down the corridors, bright lights flashing overhead, and through two swinging doors into the operating room. The ward nurse handed me over to a surgical nurse, who helped me up onto the operating table. She slid a needle in my hand as she asked about my day. What's the weather like outside? Still sunny? Have you been in an operating theatre before? She told me two instruments would be inserted in my abdomen, and my uterus, cervix and fallopian tubes would be freed and removed. There were five or six people in scrubs and masks busying themselves around the operating room. The lights were hot above me. The nurse slipped a breathing mask on my face, and soon I swam in that dark and warm place of no-thought. Parts of me I've never seen were taken away.

That term, 'freed'. It sounds so positive, as if my uterus were a rescue animal being released back into its natural habitat. I imagine opening the cage and my uterus making a break for it – the scuttling and squishy noise it makes across the linoleum floor and down the hospital corridor. When it reaches the hospital door it turns back to look at me. It's a sentimental moment: we acknowledge all the years we've spent together, and then the doors open and it disappears out onto the street.

I woke in recovery, a nurse touching my head with the back of her hand. Her skin was smooth and there was soft chatter coming from the people around us. 'Am I okay?' I asked, because I couldn't tell. I don't remember much of that evening. I was wheeled back to my room. I drifted in and out of sleep. At some point I ate dinner and talked to Jim and Sam on the phone, desperate to hear their voices. I know a nurse gave me pain relief in the middle of the night, her figure moving silently around my bed. I know that when Jim came to see me the next day I tried to make conversation but fell against him and cried in long heaving sobs. I'd been so brave. That's what the women in my family do.

/

The gynaecologist, who was also the surgeon, visited me the morning after surgery. He strode into my hospital room, a broad smile on his face. 'You look fine,' he said. The surgery had gone well and there hadn't been any cancer detected in either my cervix or my uterus. He flipped through his surgical notes. He told me that my ovaries hadn't been removed, and I felt a wash of relief at not needing hormone therapy. He paused for a moment, then said, 'Your ovaries were beautiful. They winked at me.'

To be reduced this way – to the beautiful and the coy – is to be made palatable. He did not recognise the bloodiness and complexity of what I had been through, or of womanhood. In the days before surgery I'd spent time thanking my uterus for the work it had done. The way it had built up its lining each month since I was thirteen years old, before letting the blood and tissue flow from me. For being the anchor and shelter for my son as he grew inside me. I put my hands to my stomach. 'Thanks,' I said.

My thoughts turned to a time at high school when I dubbed my best friend Melissa home on my old mountain bike. We'd been hanging around outside the local swimming pool when her period started and she didn't have a tampon. She sat balanced on my bike rack as I pedalled furiously along the leafy Ōtautahi streets, both of us laughing and yelling, but silently afraid she'd get spots of blood on her uniform. Having a period was something to hide, especially from casual passers-by. In that hospital room I also thought about the final days of pregnancy when I could feel my son push against my hands.

Of giving birth to him on the lounge floor of our small house, and after the birth – his naked body on my chest – the way the placenta slid out with a gush of fluid that soaked the carpet red. How the decision to become a parent is still seen as fundamental for women but not for men, and how that decision profoundly connects me to other women who have children, as much as it does to women who choose not to and women who can't.

/

The first few days after surgery my abdomen was swollen with gas. There were three small incisions on my lower stomach, each covered with a star of plaster strips. I could only rest on my back, as lying on my side or stomach was painful. During these days I spent most of my time in bed watching shows on my laptop or doing Sudoku. I swallowed painkillers, carefully recording the time I took each dose in a notebook so that the relief overlapped.

During that first week I dreaded bowel movements. I'd sit gingerly on the toilet and try to relax my abdominal muscles. Everything was tender and I had to take long slow breaths through pursed lips until my body took over and performed its functions. Back in bed, I pumped my feet and legs under the duvet to prevent blood clots, and got up every hour to do slow laps around our lounge and kitchen. Focusing on these small tasks helped me feel like I had some control. One friend brought me cauliflower soup, another chocolate. I reassured my parents, especially my father who was nervous about sinus surgery she was about to have, that my recovery was going fine.

I have only seen my father, Nikki, in a suit twice in my life, once at my sister's wedding and once at my own. It's strange to see her wear it – my father came out as transgender in her sixties. She is usually dressed in pretty floral tops and slacks, and always wears a blonde wig and a full face of makeup. Her fingernails are often painted pale pink and she has an enviable collection of jewellery. At Sam's birthday a few months ago the magician we'd hired asked how Nikki was related to the family. I stepped forward and introduced her as my 'parent', the best way I've found to acknowledge my father while respecting her gender identity. Without hesitation, the magician said, 'Good to meet you, love.'

It was confronting and painful to watch Nikki come out and then go through a kind of adolescence in her sixties. She wore tight red PVC dresses and long platinum blonde wigs. She posted photos of herself online, posed provocatively in lacy underwear. I understand that many trans people who come out later in life have a second adolescence like this to explore their gender identity, and I don't begrudge that to anyone. To see how the way they feel on the inside can be expressed on the outside. To find the edges of themselves.

I ask Nikki about when she first knew she was trans. 'I was about eight years old and I liked putting on my mum's fur coat,' she says. She tells me she would also read her mother's magazines, which 'were full of lovely-looking 1950s women'. My father grew up in 1950s Ravensbourne, a suburb in Ōtepoti. Her own father was a butcher, and her mother an elegant woman who ruled their household. My father didn't yet know what being transgender was. She didn't know how she was different.

When I ask Nikki why it took her so long to come out, she says, 'The main thing in my life back then was the pressure from my mum to do well at school. My dad, although a lovely kind person who worked hard to support us, was not the role model my mum wanted for me. I suppose what I am trying to say is that often your identity is subsumed under other pressures. I think that has been the pattern in my life.'

/

During my recovery I watched the Netflix special *Nanette* by comedian Hannah Gadsby, a deeply funny, political and heart-breaking account of Gadsby's experience of being 'not normal'. As a woman and lesbian who lives in a fat body and has a traditional masculine appearance, Gadsby reports that people often see her as being 'incorrectly female', and that she is persecuted for her otherness. With unflinching directness, Gadsby talks of being beaten by a man because she was a 'lady faggot', of being sexually abused as a child, and of being raped by two men in her twenties.[9] And worse than these assaults? The shame and self-hatred she carries.

Nikki and I last argued about womanhood when she proudly showed me an airbrushed photo of herself. We were in my parents' study in their house in Ōtautahi, which is also the house I grew up in. I'd flown down for work and was staying the night with my parents. She handed me a colour printout of the photo, and the blonde ingénue staring back at me looked to be in her early twenties. She had smooth skin and strawberry lips, her face cheeky and inviting. I was marking my students' creative writing assignments at the time, my hair dragged back in a ponytail, wearing a baggy t-shirt and track pants. 'Stop buying into this beauty bullshit,' I said, suddenly angry. I pointed to my greasy-haired, no-makeup appearance. 'Am I less of a woman?' I asked. Dad looked crestfallen. 'But you're always beautiful,' she said.

I know I have internalised my father's ideas about womanhood, which are really not hers at all but Western society's gender norms. I don't think it's a stretch to say they're a type of trauma. A 'transmittable encultured process' is how social scientist Meera Atkinson describes my inheritance.[10] Atkinson's research looks at how patriarchy creates trauma and then passes it to the next generation. She draws a disturbing image when she writes that, wherever patriarchy exists,

gardens of grandeur have grown on the blood and bone of
subjugated women, children, slaves, invaded and colonised
peoples, and nonhuman animals. In other words, conceiving
of trauma as a structural force uncovers the way it informs
racism, sexism, homophobia, colonialism.[11]

In that moment in the study I wish I'd had more empathy for my father. I hadn't watched *Beauty* by YouTuber, political commentator and trans woman Natalie Wynn.[12] I hadn't learned about the way many trans people want to pass and feel beautiful to lessen their gender dysphoria, to feel safe in public spaces and sometimes because of their own internalised transphobia. I also hadn't read Alok Vaid-Menon, who eloquently describes the way 'the experiences of White, middleclass, cisgender straight women are taken as the default experience for all women' so that trans people often experience 'trans misogyny', where their bodies are constantly scrutinised and judged as if there's something fundamentally wrong with them.[13] My reaction to my father brings to mind Maggie Nelson, who, in *The Argonauts*, describes fearing the physical changes that will happen when her spouse Harry starts taking testosterone. She panic-suggests they should focus on 'internal' change instead. 'As if I did not know that, in the field of gender, there is no charting where the external and the internal begin and end', Nelson admits.[14]

Arguing with my father that day, I felt possessive of womanhood. I felt she was getting it all wrong. But Nikki never got the chance in her twenties to live as a woman – to party and wear short dresses and sleep with strangers as I did, or to express her youth in other ways. To feel erotic and feminine and powerful. She never had the chance to learn that feeling desired and valuable can come from other parts of ourselves; that those feelings have nothing to do with how we look, even though we are told otherwise. At age thirty Dad was still searching the local library to find out who she was.

Late one evening, a few weeks after surgery, I finally understood that my uterus was gone. A huge wave of panic swelled in my stomach as I realised I couldn't get it back. Where was it? Was it in some biological waste disposal unit? I imagined my uterus scrabbling at the sides of a plastic bin in the dark.

The next day, at my request, the gynaecologist sent me a picture of my uterus taken by the technician who did the biopsy. I clicked on the email attachment and the image filled my screen. An organ against a tan background. In the photo my uterus looks like it's dancing: blueish fallopian tubes undulate from the reddish mass of the womb. Even though the image was taken from above, my uterus appears as though it's standing, balanced on the thick white plug of my cervix. I immediately loved this strange and beautiful animal. Even though it's gone, it will always be part of the first forty years of my womanhood, and I'm grateful that for a time it was inside me. That afternoon I sent an email to update my father on my recovery. The subject line: 'Today we are both women without a uterus'.

/

In her essay 'Mothers as Makers of Death', on the difficulty of being a mother and a writer, Claudia Dey states: 'To write is to be in conversation with yourself, to preserve a state of being so you can conclude a sequence of thinking and feeling.'[15] This book is a conversation with myself about my own womanhood. Because, in the end, I lied to my gynaecologist when I told him I knew what made up my womanhood. Until I had a hysterectomy I had not seriously thought about what womanhood meant. I couldn't answer the question, 'What is my womanhood?' without leaning on cisgender biological descriptions or framing womanhood in opposition to maleness. I felt like all my answers were the hollow recitations of what I had been taught and told. I knew my womanhood was warm and life-giving, but it was like sunlight cutting shapes across a wall: I could not reach out my hand and grasp it.

To write this book I pulled on the thread of my womanhood to see how it unravelled. And how quickly it did. The act of looking showed me the stitches: Western society's beauty standards, the male gaze, a fear of ageing, hair and gender, care work, my grandmother, life-stage transitions, orca whales and tramping. All the people whose works I explored – Darcey Steinke, Alok Vaid-Menon, Megan Jayne Crabbe, Maggie Nelson, Reni Eddo-Lodge, Judith Butler, Barbara Brookes, Natalie Wynn, Ani Mikaere, Atul Gawande and many more – offered up ideas about gender, ageing and society in a way that opened a door to the next idea. I kept on walking through those doors. The result is what I am calling my 'coming-of-middle-age' story. I have tried to understand which parts of womanhood are mine, which have been given to me, and out of them all, which I want to keep.

I found it difficult to write this book in an instinctive way. My academic training wanted me to weigh up all the different arguments, whereas my gut told me to follow the research paths that *felt* right. I spent my first forty years ignoring what *felt* right and instead chose to listen to other people, so working this way was uncomfortable. Was *feeling things* a defendable methodology? I worried about the way my story would, through the nature of it being mine, exclude lots of other experiences of womanhood, especially non-Pākehā experiences. I worried that I couldn't read everything. That no matter how much research I did there would be theories and writers I'd missed. I didn't want my experience to stand in for a multitude of women's experiences, as can often happen when work is in the public sphere. Mostly I worried that I'd get it all wrong. My fears were an embodied illustration of the way I'd been taught not to value my voice, and I fought them fiercely.

Another choice that shaped the book was a promise I made to myself to primarily use resources that could freely be found online or in a public library. I couldn't afford to buy academic articles, magazine subscriptions and shelves of new books, and I wanted to make sure curious readers didn't have to either. The goal of this book is to help other women, in some small way, think about their own womanhood, and, beyond the offer of my own experience, anyone should be able to read through my reference list if they want.

Because the book is written as an unpicking of my womanhood, it has a particular focus on what it means to be middle-aged. I couldn't have written this book before now because as a younger woman I was in thrall to society's ideal womanhood. I wanted nothing more than to be that perfect woman, because being perfect meant being safe. And as a conventionally attractive, educated, Pākehā woman I could often get close to (and benefit from) that ideal. I was one of the 'good' ones and was praised for how dedicated I was in my self-devastation. Like many women in emotionally abusive relationships, I protected and defended my abuser.

My failure to meet society's ideal womanhood has brought me here. Since entering my forties I have become fatter, dimplier and more wrinkled. I have greying hair and thicker arms. My face has relaxed; time has shaped my features. I can no longer reproduce because I have no uterus. I would also like to think that I am better at being myself. This natural and normal ageing process has made me increasingly invisible and irrelevant in societal terms, and I expect that to continue. But entering middle age has given me a clearer understanding of gender norms. It let me see how much of my self-worth and identity were wedded to being that hungry and quiet young woman. Failure was my salvation, because it made me work to see the mechanics of my womanhood. In seeing, choice became possible.

This book is also the work and product of a particular zeitgeist, that of the first decades of the twenty-first century and the necessary earthquakes of the #MeToo movement, Black Lives Matter, LGBTQIA+ rights, and intersectional and trans-inclusive feminism. I'm not an expert in any of these topics – I am simply a person trying to understand what it is to live well in these places. There is no lack of experts though, and I hope this book honours their voices. I hope that it will start conversations for women, both in the gentle rooms of ourselves and with each other.

Chapter Two

I miss your pussy

We drive down the hill to the local school with its wide expanse of basketball courts. It's the weekend, so the yellow-lined concrete stretches empty before us. We're here so Sam can learn to ride his bike without training wheels, which he hasn't wanted to do until now. He's nearly eight, and we're in negotiation – he wants to put the training wheels back on. He stands in the middle of the court, grey hoodie zipped up to his chin, and tells me in a serious voice that he doesn't care that he can't ride without them. He only wants to ride along the waterfront, and maybe around his school, and training wheels are fine for that. 'Come on, Ma,' he says.

I try to explain that just like he's learned to swim and to tie his shoelaces, he needs to learn to ride his bike. I tell him it's an essential life skill. He cocks his head to one side in suspicion. When his dad first came to Aotearoa New Zealand he biked around the North Island, I say. What if he wants to do something like that when he's older? I imagine future-him setting off, his belongings folded into a yellow pannier and me waving goodbye from the kerb. But he's not with me. His eyes have gone to a man and a toddler playing on the green sports field. 'Let's make a deal,' I say. 'Let's try this one time without training wheels and if it doesn't work I'll put them back on.'

We get into position at one end of the courts, and I kneel down to buckle his helmet. I tuck a piece of hair out of his eyes. Sam straddles the bike. 'Don't let go until I tell you,' he says, and his eyes meet mine. He begins to push down on the pedals and I put my hands to his small waist. I don't know what I'm doing, but I run beside him, hunched slightly, my hands trying to hold him. He starts to pedal faster and gets a rhythm going, and now I'm really running, my trainers pounding the ground as one of my hands lifts away, the other just touching, and I can tell he's doing it, his body upright and balanced, his legs pushing forward in fluid strokes, and then he yells, 'Let go!'

The day Sam first rides his bike is around a year after I have my hysterectomy. I am forty-one. Not long after, I go into central Te Whanganui-a-Tara to buy a new pair of running shoes – the same brand I've bought every year for at least a decade. I've been a runner since my early twenties. There have been long sunrise runs around the Miramar Peninsula and out-and-back suburban runs on weekday mornings. Whenever I travel, I map out a new run in the city where I'm staying. I started running after an important relationship ended. A reinvention. A taking back of my body. Now when I run I feel most like myself.

In the brightly lit store, shoes line the walls, each sitting on its own platform. I find my shoe and turn it over in my hands – this year the design is navy blue and silver, which I like better than last year's pink. A young man who works at the store spots me and heads over. 'The Adrenaline! Nice choice,' he says. He starts to talk about the mechanics of the shoe, the sole construction and pronation support. 'I know,' I say, feeling awkward. As I slip the shoe on, he kneels down and shows me how to thread the laces: over, over, under.

I watch his hands flash across my foot. At the checkout he gives me a complimentary bottle of water and asks why I've decided to start running. I feel my face get hot. I explain that I've been running for twenty years. That, over that time, I've run around 20,000 kilometres. That I've done a marathon and half-marathons. He nods and smiles while ringing up the shoes. 'Yeah, my mum likes to run,' he says.

In that moment, likened to a young man's mother, I knew I'd passed from young adulthood into middle age. Unlike the transitions of my childhood – the first day of school, my first tentative kiss, or even the first time I rode my bike – I didn't see this one coming. I'd never thought that much about what it would mean to be middle-aged. I was not prepared for it. With a combination of denial and magical thinking, I had assumed that I'd be a young adult for about sixty years before I slid right into revered elderliness. Driving home, my heart beat wildly. To be middle-aged was to be unattractive, dumpy and slow, right? To be middle-aged as a woman – well, that was to be forever compared unfavourably with my younger self. To disappear into her shadow.

After Sam rode his bike that day we walked back to our car and he insisted on helping me lift the bike into the boot. He had a small smile on his face, and I could tell he was proud of himself. 'What's next?' he asked as he leaned into me, childhood spreading before him, one small arm wrapped around my waist.

/

I remember seeing a black-and-white photograph of my father at primary school in Ōtepoti in the early 1950s. Her face looked older than I expected. It was as though an adult's head had been collaged onto a child's body, and the weight of that adultness gave my father a strange bobblehead appearance. Robert Pogue Harrison, who writes about the way society sees ageing, had a similar thought when he looked at photographs of his father, saying 'twelve-year-old boys looked like little adults, their faces furrowed by the depths of time'.[1]

Years of concentration have etched lines across my forehead so even when I'm not frowning it resembles a Venetian blind. Recently, I've noticed lines forming at the edges of my mouth and up from the bow of my lip. Fine contour lines extend from my eyes and down my cheekbones like animal tracks down a hill. Still, my face has a youthfulness that my great-grandparents didn't have in their forties. While some of this could be genetics, the main reason is probably because I live in a culture and country where youthfulness has been extended for around 80 percent of the population – or in other words, for those of us who do not live in poverty.[2] For the segment of the population I'm part of, our food is mostly nutritious, most of us work indoors, and we have ready access to sunscreen, medication and labour-saving technologies. These advantages have created a society that Harrison refers to as 'younger in looks, behaviour, mentality, lifestyles, and above all, desires' than any other in human history.[3]

While an extended period of youthfulness may mean we're in better physical health than the generations who came before, it has also created an expectation that we will remain forever young, and consequently a fear of ageing. British psychologist Dr Eileen Bradbury, who coined the term 'permayouth', explains how our expectation that we will remain youthful means we often resort to plastic surgery to get closer to how we think we should look.[4] We are taught to look back on our younger selves with a sense of longing and loss and then directed to products that only increase that yearning.[5]

Over the years I have tried to erase the history of my own ageing. I have polished, exfoliated, promoted cell growth, infused my skin with ultrasonic energy, exposed my face to wavelengths of light, dyed, contoured, reduced, refined, reshaped, slimmed, firmed, hydrated, sculpted, smoothed, controlled and targeted myself with a refreshing cream-gel that instantly absorbs. When I turned forty, I signed up for a 'Skin Health Membership' at a local beauty chain, which had nothing to do with 'health' but involved an anti-ageing facial every three weeks. I told the beauty therapist that, at forty, I had decided to take better care of my skin. I said that I wanted to pamper myself a little. I gave the same reason to my friends and Jim, and to myself.

For the first treatment I arrived early, sat in the airy foyer and drank the complimentary spring water. On the glass coffee table was a fan of beauty magazines, and calming classical music was piped from an invisible speaker. The beauty therapist came out of the long corridor that I guessed led to the treatment rooms. She wore a neat black uniform and had a huge mass of curly red hair. I followed her to a room where she explained we were going to focus our appointments on microdermabrasion and glycolic acid peels – they were best for a woman my age. 'Soon you'll look ten years younger,' she said.

Over the next few months we alternated between the two treatments. During microdermabrasion, the beauty therapist used a small vacuum tube to sand away the surface of my face with tiny particles of aluminium oxide. She started at my forehead and made her way down my cheeks and along my jawline in hard feathered strokes. I held my face still, my eyes closed. It felt as though tiny needles were being pricked into my skin. A strange, almost out-of-body feeling came over me. *How had I ended up here?* As she moved across my face, she talked about how her boyfriend always worked weekends, which she found hard. She told me how she'd moved out of home because she didn't get on with her stepmother, and about the parties she went to. She was friendly and chatty. I liked the beauty therapist.

She used glycolic acid for a similar skin-stripping effect. After cleansing, she painted my face with the acid using firm strokes of a long-handled brush, and then massaged the acid into my skin, her fingertips moving in small circular movements. Years ago, when I was prone to anxiety attacks, a therapist recommended that when an attack came on I take an ice cube from the freezer and squeeze it in the palm of my hand. The shock of the pain and cold was meant to distract me from the pulsing anxiety and ground me back into my body. The acid on my face felt like clutching that ice. I wondered what I was being brought back to, or what I was distracting myself from.

As the months went on, I started to dread going to appointments. I would drive to the clinic with a clenched feeling in my throat. When summer came, I scheduled a long break from the treatments, using the excuse of the school holidays. When the treatments started again, I vowed to cancel my membership, but found myself unable to say those words to the smiling receptionist. I'd leave with the next appointment booked. While at some level my body knew that what I was doing to my face was a type of violence, a louder part of me felt afraid to stop. It was as though two women were living inside me.

Looking back, I can see my experience is typical of the way beauty standards are used for commercial gain. The convincing and well-informed therapists, the tasteful vase of lilies at reception, the shelves of exclusive skin care, the photographs of line-free women smiling on the walls with slogans such as 'Look your best version of fresh' – they all told me ageing was disgraceful. It's hard to speak up in such an environment, to be the single stick that stops a wheel.

Eventually I did cancel my membership. I didn't tell my beauty therapist that it was because I felt the treatments undermined my self-worth – that I'd realised they were a mistake and I wanted to appreciate my face as it aged. I felt ashamed of the months I'd spent pretending, and of how much money I'd wasted. Instead, I told her I was having 'financial difficulties' and would come back after things were better. She nodded understandingly, her red curls bouncing, and then started to talk about my lip lines. 'When you come back, we could easily do fillers,' she said. She told me how, at twenty-one, she'd started regular Botox injections as a way to prevent wrinkles forming. She'd never need fillers. She turned her dewy forehead up to the light. 'I was lucky to start early,' she said.

Writing this now, I watch a video on YouTube of a woman having fillers. She is reclined in what looks like a dentist's chair, her face smooth and expressionless. The American-accented voiceover talks about contours and gels and sculpting. Starting at the corner of the woman's mouth, a beautician slides a needle into the border of her lips. She works her way along the upper lip line, injecting filler under the skin. Small spheres of blood well up where the needle has been. They remind me of the bright red rosary beads that are often hung on statues of the Virgin Mary. In the Catholic faith, the red represents redemption through eternal life. In a way, the act does seem like a prayer – a painful and desperate plea.

/

When I signed up for skin treatments, I had just read *Body Positive Power* by activist Megan Jayne Crabbe. In her book, Crabbe writes about the way fashion companies, for financial gain, have deliberately created an ideal woman through their narrow selection of models. Crabbe describes this woman as 'thin, white, beautiful, young, [and] able' (to which I would add cisgender and heteronormative).[6] Fashion images are manipulated so all signs of ageing are erased. While young women struggle to meet the ideal, virtually no woman over the age of fifty can because '"Beauty" is also a code word for youth'.[7]

So I knew that the way society idolises youth damages women (which is unlikely to be news to anyone reading this book). I considered myself an ally of the body positivity movement. It's perplexing for me that the woman who is writing this book is the same woman who paid to have acid stroked over her face. But I think that's why I'm writing: there's no simple answer.

Around the time my body started to noticeably age, I went out to meet a friend for lunch. I decided to wear an orange-and-blue checked coat that I hadn't put on since the previous winter. The bright pattern made it one of my favourite items of clothing, and it stood out on the wintery Te Whanganui-a-Tara streets. That morning, as I tried to pull on the coat, it felt different – it was tight across my arms and shoulders, which are the places I've always put on weight. I struggled out of the sleeves and stuffed the coat back into my closet.

Over the next few days I unpicked the shoulder and arm seams of the coat. I carefully cut out the silky lining, let the seams out and sewed the coat back together. I did this in secret, behind a closed door. I didn't want Jim or Sam to ask what I was doing, even though they must have heard the sewing machine. I told myself that I was altering the coat because it was pure wool and it had been expensive. I was being frugal because colourful coats like this were hard to find. I knew the truth was that a part of me expected to continue to fit the coat, even though my mother had bought it for me ten years earlier. That I expected, *needed*, my body to remain the same, even after a decade of ageing and having a child and a hysterectomy. My hypocrisy became clear. It had been easy to be 'body positive' when I lived in a thin young body. *Had my beliefs been false? How could I be so treacherous?* All I knew was the ill-fitting coat was somehow my failure.

The body positivity movement originated in Black feminism and 'the feminist and "black is beautiful" movements of the 1960s'.[8] Black fat activists advocated for fat bodies and drew attention to the intersection of size discrimination with other discriminations based on race and gender. The early movement encouraged Black women to 'shed ideas of beauty predicated on whiteness' and redefine for themselves what an acceptable body looked like.[9] In 1967, Lew Louderback published the essay 'More People Should Be FAT', which led, in 1969, to the formation of the American organisation the National Association to Advance Fat Acceptance (originally called the National Association to Aid Fat Americans). Fat acceptance activists argue for a Health at Every Size (HAES) approach where fatness is not an indicator of poor health, and dieting is seen as having negative mental health outcomes. In 1978, *Fat Is a Feminist Issue* by Susie Orbach was one of the first books to explore women's relationships with food, eating and their bodies. The history of thought on this issue is now long.

As a Pākehā girl growing up in Ōtautahi, my first inkling that there was a feminist perspective on women's bodies and beauty came after the 1990 publication of Naomi Wolf's *The Beauty Myth*. Although I didn't read the book until recently, Wolf's ideas seeped into mainstream culture and my teen consciousness. In *The Beauty Myth*, Wolf argues that beauty ideals serve to undermine women's financial, social and political progress by encouraging women to see their value as inherently linked to their beauty, therefore making us preoccupied with our appearance. As Wolf says, 'women's identity must be premised upon our "beauty" so that we will remain vulnerable to outside approval.'[10] If women are constantly concerned with beauty and approval, we are less able to participate in areas of consequence: politics, media, art, medicine, academia, social justice and activism – the realms of power.

It has been over thirty years since *The Beauty Myth* came out. In an updated introduction in 2002, Wolf noted that beauty standards have started to apply to other genders. A greater proportion of men are having plastic surgery – a clear sign, she says, that men are no longer the 'arbiters' of beauty but have joined the victims.[11] But, Wolf wonders, is it 'progress when both genders can be commodified and evaluated as objects?'[12] Wolf again updated her introduction in 2015, noting that fourth- and fifth-wave feminists are more educated 'about the intersection of race, class and gender' as well as LGBTQIA+ rights than previous waves but that the issues she wrote about in 1990 are still, for the most part, present, including women's fear of ageing.[13]

As with many books and movies from the late twentieth century, *The Beauty Myth* has been reassessed by more than Wolf's new introductions. In her essay 'A Modern Feminist Classic Changed My Life. Was It Actually Garbage?', Rebecca Onion rereads *The Beauty Myth* on its thirtieth anniversary.[14] In its pages Onion finds equal amounts of 'thought experiments gone wrong'[15] and 'clunky bits of analysis using race'[16] alongside the poignant and useful pieces she remembers. In recent years, Wolf has turned conspiracy theorist – she is a Covid-truther and antivaxxer who believes among other theories, that clouds are manufactured – and Onion sees tendencies towards conspiracy in *The Beauty Myth*. Wolf seems to believe there is a 'superstructure' that purposefully manipulates society in order to control women,[17] but Onion disagrees such a structure exists, as do I.

Despite the manufactured clouds, I value Wolf's touching passages about ageing, and the impact her book had at the time. And the fact *The Beauty Myth* is being reassessed is a sure sign we're moving forward. Over the last sixty years in particular, society's awareness of the mechanics and damage of beauty ideals (and how they intersect with race, gender and other discrimination) has expanded from niche, primarily Black feminist groups to mainstream awareness. I think a sign that the movement has become mainstream is its appropriation by companies to sell products – Dove's 2004 Self-Esteem Project or the *Yoga Journal*'s 'Body Issue' in 2014 are two campaigns that use the language of body positivity (but have been criticised for depoliticising and whitewashing the movement, and using it for commercial gain).[18]

As I write this, #bodypositivity has nearly 6 million posts on Instagram, which is due to the work of activists such as Stephanie Yeboah, Tess Holliday, Jessamyn Stanley, Christy Harrison, the EveryMAN project and the many others who create online spaces for body positivity, body acceptance and HAES. I have seen this activism start to influence people in positions of power. One instance that comes to mind is when, in 2016, London mayor Sadiq Khan banned Protein World's 'Are you beach body ready?' advertising campaign from public transport. The advertisements featured a thin, young, able-bodied, Caucasian and bikini-clad model, and Khan said that he felt this type of advertising 'can demean people, particularly women, and make them ashamed of their bodies'.[19]

While no doubt we have come a long way, I do worry it's mainly happening in a passionately feminist echo chamber. That in changing how the wider culture views women's bodies, women have been given a Sisyphean task. Most of the imagery I see of women – on websites, billboards and in magazines – still celebrates youthful thinness. The other morning, while driving through the city, I passed an advertising poster showing a thin, young, bikini-clad Pākehā woman rising out of four colourful inflatable rings. She was at the beach. Her eyes were closed, her head tilted backward and she was touching her face suggestively. 'Taste the feeling,' the advert said. When I find myself in a group of women not directly involved or interested in body positivity or HAES, the conversation often turns to 'goal weights' and 'clean eating'. If the women are over forty, the conversation inevitably becomes one about appearance and ageing.

Recently I was at a pub with a group of women in their mid-forties. One lamented that ageing meant she would no longer be attractive to men. Not men who were younger than her, but *all* men. We were spread over a couple of tables, our conversations jumping quickly between topics. There was a band playing music in the background and everyone was giddy after a few glasses of wine. I didn't try to talk to my friend about what she'd said. It was too noisy and it wasn't the right time. But as I sat on that uncomfortable pub seat my heart ached for her. I guessed what she was really saying was that she felt scared. I often felt a similar feathery fear creep over me. I felt like she was asking, 'Who am I if I'm no longer desirable?' *Would she even exist?*

What I think women fear losing is the value we are afforded by the 'male gaze', a phrase that has become well known since it was first used by Laura Mulvey in her 1975 essay 'Visual Pleasure and Narrative Cinema'.[20] Since then, the term has broken free from the realms of film criticism to more broadly represent the patriarchal objectification of women. The male gaze reduces women from people with full and individuated selves to archetypes without complexity or agency: women become submissive and passive; maternal and self-sacrificing; or whoreish and sexually welcoming. In feminist theory, the male gaze is seen as active and is underpinned with the 'real social power' that men possess.[21] Women do not get such power: because the male gaze reduces them to roles where they are passive or exist only for men's pleasure, women cannot gaze back. The gaze wipes away their humanity and individuality. The pervasiveness of the male gaze in how women are portrayed combined with men's social power means that women often come to believe that these meagre and denigrating narratives *are* womanhood.[22] As John Berger writes in *Ways of Seeing*, '*men act* and *women appear*. Men look at women. Women watch themselves being looked at.'[23] This dynamic of seeing and being seen influences relationships between men and women, and also a woman's relationship with herself. We end up believing that to be a woman is to rise suggestively in a bikini from the sea.

Philosopher Mary Devereaux suggests that the male gaze is both literal and figurative, and I have found this description useful in understanding how it works in my life. She writes that 'in literal terms, the gaze is male when men do the looking' but that figuratively the male gaze refers to 'a way of seeing which takes women as its object'.[24] The conflation of the two is one of the problems brought about by the popularity of the phrase, because the male gaze is often taken to mean there is always a man doing the gazing. While the literal use does mean there is a man seeing a woman as an object, the figurative use applies to anywhere where the norms and values are traditionally male and dictate narrow ideas of womanhood.

It's probably no surprise that the beauty clinic I went to was staffed entirely by women, who saw women's appearance and ageing through the male gaze even though no individual man was present to do the gazing (although I learned later that the owner and person who benefited financially from the clinic was a man). What brought me to the beauty clinic was me turning an inner male gaze upon myself, an act which Berger describes as happening when '[t]he surveyor of woman in herself is male'.[25] Queer women are also affected by the pressures of the societal male gaze, even if they have no interest in being gazed upon by men as sexual or romantic partners.

The dynamic traps men too. Otherwise kind and progressive men use the male gaze, which they have internalised like the rest of us. And men themselves suffer under the male gaze, by either hiding aspects of themselves that are considered traditionally feminine or by being abused for them. Picking up Sam and his male friend from school the other day, I found his friend in tears. He was standing at the edge of the playground, back turned to the after-school basketball game. When I asked him what happened he told me that one of the older girls was picking on him because he likes to wear his hair in a ponytail. Head bowed, he said, 'She called me a rrrrl.' I bent down and asked him to repeat what he said. 'A *girl*,' he said, and glared up at me with red-rimmed eyes. 'She keeps on calling me a girl.' Some days it feels like we've come a long way since the popularity of 'sissy' as an insult, and other days it doesn't.

All of that said, both the literal and figurative male gaze emerge from a society where White men have long dominated positions of power, and contemporary men benefit from the legacy of that power. Some of the most damaging and long-lasting lessons I've learned (and then had to painfully unlearn) about my value as a woman came from boys and men.

I'm in high school and I'm lying on my childhood bed with an older boy. Let's call him C. I must be about fifteen. I can't remember if we'd walked to my house after school or if we're on a study break, but I know that I'm wearing my school uniform. C is on the same sports team as me but he's a better athlete than I am; he's in a higher grade. I think he's cool. My bedroom has a large bay window that looks out over a rhododendron garden. The blooms are massive and opulent. Snowy white and buttery yellow flowers filter the afternoon sun as we lie close together on my single bed. Brown hair, brown eyes. He slides one tanned hand across my waist and untucks my white shirt from my kilt. An excited shiver runs up my neck. 'Let's see,' he says as he slides the shirt off my stomach. He takes my skin between his thumb and index finger and pinches it. He gives my flesh a small wiggle. 'Pretty good,' he says, but then leans closer and moves to another spot. He pinches and wiggles again. 'Nope, you've got some fat here,' he says.

It's a few months into my third year of art school, and I've just had sex with S, who is also at art school. We're both twenty. That night we'd been out playing pool with some friends and I'd worn a new green dress. It's one that I'd made myself, copying the design from a magazine and running it up on my old sewing machine. Wearing the dress I feel sexy. That night we'd circled each other around the pool table in the hazy lounge. He didn't look at me often, and instead talked to our friends and slowly drunk his beer. I knew he was pretending to ignore me because every now and then, when I bent to take a shot, he'd glance over. Now I'm lying naked in his bed in the half-light. The room has a muggy tang from us. He goes to the window and opens it wide into the night. He sits on the windowsill and lights a cigarette, its orange tip flaring in the darkness. 'That short dress,' he says and laughs and shakes his head. He isn't looking at me but out into the night. 'I don't usually have sex with chunky girls,' he says. He turns to face me. 'It wasn't that bad.'

I'm older now. My boyfriend and I have been together for three years, but things aren't going well. We're sitting on his couch eating dinner from our laps and watching a movie. On screen a man and a woman are having sex. It's very theatrical – the woman is on top of her lover, throwing her head about and arching her back. 'That's one of my favourites,' my boyfriend says, referring to the position. He gestures a forkful of bolognese towards the screen before putting it in his mouth. 'When you lean right back, your stomach becomes taut. Like a porn star,' he says. Months after we break up and while still irrational with grief, I send him a message: 'I miss you.' His response: 'I miss your pussy. Whenever a woman parts her legs for me I'm disappointed.'

These memories have stayed with me over the years. In a way they are minor and fleeting – they don't describe workplace harassment or sexual assault, although I have those stories as well, as most women do. These stories feel powerful to me because they are so common and everyday, and they each happened with a person I trusted, at least well enough to be sexually intimate with. And intimacy made me vulnerable to the other person's view of who I was and who I should be. That's the insidiousness of the male gaze – these boys and men saw their use and objectification of me as normal and acceptable, and for a long time I believed it was acceptable too.

/

It doesn't surprise me then that my friend in the pub fears ageing – I think she's seeing herself through the male gaze. As a monogamous and married woman, she is probably not worried about the literal male gaze and her ability to find a partner (although as another friend points out, older women are regularly left for younger women). I think she's worried that ageing will mean she'll lose her value, both for herself and others, which limits who she can be. And although we live in a society that has been positively shaped by waves of feminism – I can vote, work, dress, speak and love more freely than the women who've lived before me – the issue of how women are valued lives on.

I ask my friend Nicola what she thinks about ageing and limits. She's a music professor at a liberal arts college in the United States, as well as a concert pianist. She's one of the few women I know who does not link her value with how she looks, but she's just come out of a twelve-year relationship. 'I'm ready for questions about dating as a middle-aged woman,' she says when we get on the Zoom call. 'Tell me all about it,' I say. She nods and sips her tea and looks serious. 'Ageing has been sneaky,' she says. 'When you're in a relationship for twelve years you assume that person understands who you are and has watched you age. You don't notice people ageing when you're with them. Suddenly I've had to shift that gaze back at myself and ask how I seem to other people. I've never thought of myself as a vain person, but suddenly I have anxiety about how I look.' I ask her if that anxiety comes from dating again. 'Part of the anger of coming out of that relationship was feeling like my options are smaller because I'm fifty-six,' she says. 'You can't just be an older version of the attractive younger person you once were,' she says, and we laugh a while about the term 'cougar'. 'The fact is, though, an attractive woman in her fifties is so surprising she needs a label,' Nicola says. 'At some point a switch is flipped because of your age and you are no longer seen as viable, even to a man the same age as you.' She pauses for a moment. 'People don't write guidebooks for being a woman at fifty-six and by yourself. And I feel like I'm coming up on a pretty powerful part of my life.'

In her essay 'The Invisibility of Older Women' Akiko Busch, paraphrasing Alison Carper, writes that we all know, to the point of cliché, the way men objectify women, but that women also objectify themselves. And when a woman treats herself as an object she becomes keenly aware when that object is no longer desirable.[26] A 2017 study in the *Journal of Women & Aging* shows that almost all women objectify themselves and that body positive activists are the outliers. Respondents to the study – nearly 2000 women over fifty who live in the United States – were ashamed of the changes happening to their body as they aged, such as a thickening of the fat layer through the torso, and loose and wrinkled skin. A significant number of the women admitted to 'eating disorder symptoms, and extreme weight control methods' to try to counter the signs of ageing.[27] Although respondents reported that they saw older women portrayed in the media, they felt those women 'were rarely being authentic and presenting their true appearance' and their pictures were 'commonly doctored to erase visible signs of aging'.[28] I know that when I see world-famous women such as Dame Helen Mirren and Julianne Moore glittering on my screen, I don't see them as role models for my own ageing. Their aged beauty feels entirely out of reach.

For the women in the study there was a feeling of 'irrelevance and invisibility' that came upon them as they aged, and an expectation that they would accept that invisibility.[29] This sense that others see you as irrelevant can be especially strong for women without children. Dorthe Nors, who writes novels about the lives of middle-aged women, says: 'If a woman has kids, she will always be a mother, but a woman who has chosen not to procreate and who now no longer is young and sexy is perceived by many as a pointless being.'[30] On the flipside, women who choose to become mothers are among the most disempowered as we age when it comes to earning potential (a phenomenon called the 'motherhood penalty') and are also the most burdened by unpaid care work.[31]

Reading Nors' words I am reminded of the young man in the shoe store who compared me to his mother. What other archetypes did he have available to him? The figures of 'maiden', 'mother' and 'crone' seem woefully inadequate to capture womanhood in the twenty-first century (and if those are what he had to hand, in hindsight mother seems like a safe bet). To ask a better question – what stories of womanhood and midlife do women have available to us? How do we create these stories ourselves?

When I hear the fear and confusion in my friend's voice, I recognise it in myself. I've had the privilege to grow up acceptably feminine with my long hair and a slimmish body. I am grateful to have married a man who continues to find me beautiful as my body and face change over the years; Jim tells me my beauty emanates from inside of me. As part of our wedding vows we promised each other that we would stay 'age-appropriately hot', which was meant to be funny, but it was also a way to acknowledge to each other that our bodies will change and that it's okay.

Women who have lived their whole lives outside of the beauty ideal – gender non-conforming women, women who are fat or whiskered or whose skin is deemed too dark, who use wheelchairs or hearing aids, who have lost a limb or who have acne or scars – will have an experience different to and more difficult than mine. At the same time, we share much. Because, even for someone like me, whose social media feed is full of women of varied sizes and ages loving their bodies, who is the 'go-to' one for feminist issues at work, who has spent decades learning intuitive eating and ways to quieten my own internalised male gaze and who is writing this book – on bad days even I end up in a beauty therapist's chair or standing in front of a mirror and pinching my stomach to decide my worth.

Chapter Three
Making gender trouble

When I think about power and womanhood, I think of my grandmother Sheila. She never had the sort of power that money could afford, but if you happened to be in the cosy lounge of her retirement flat and she told you to sit, you'd feel yourself move to her floral couch to sit down. It's not that people were afraid of her. Sheila just had an unarguable sureness of her own worth and her right to be heard. People were also drawn to her kindness. When my infant son met her for the first time, she drew him onto her lap. They were sitting on the narrow bench outside her flat. She looped one arthritic arm around him and let him pull on the loose skin of her face. She talked away to him softly. I took a photograph of the two of them – her wrapped in a purple cardigan against the English autumn, my son staring intensely at her aged face.

Although Sheila was kind, she often had a sharp tongue. On one visit when I was in my mid-twenties she suddenly turned to me, probably prompted by my self-absorbed moaning, and scolded me for ruining my first marriage. She was not wrong, but I was so hurt and ashamed that I walked out of her flat and along the leafy canal back to my aunt and uncle's house, where I was staying. Later that evening the phone rang; she'd called to apologise. While all was mended, I was reminded of the family saying: 'Grandma doesn't suffer fools.' I think that especially applied to foolish young women who wouldn't take responsibility for their own lives.

Sheila's stoicism was no doubt because of her childhood. Sheila was born in 1918 in Hednesford, a small town in the English West Midlands. She lived with her family in a flat above the bakery run by her father, and her grandfather lived with them as well. She had many relatives in nearby towns and she'd often visit them with her mother. Her family were working-class – seamstresses and miners – and while they were not living in poverty, there wasn't much extra to spare. It was common for one family to move in with another when times were hard. After her father lost the bakery during the Great Depression, the whole family moved in with his parents until he could raise enough money to buy another business. When the house Sheila was born in was pulled down for pit work, her mother showed her the empty space, as if to say there's no reason to be sentimental about these sorts of things.

Childhood gave Sheila an inner resolve, but I don't want to fetishise hardship. There were many opportunities that my grand-mother didn't have because she was working-class. Her parents couldn't afford to send her to university so instead Sheila left school at seventeen and sat the Civil Service exam. During World War II she worked at Telephone House in Birmingham. Her offices were located at the top of the building, and she worried constantly that they would be bombed. Each day she would get the bus to Coseley Station, a train to Birmingham and then walk to work through the jagged rubble of buildings bombed the night before.

Sheila met and married her husband Len before the war, but he was soon deployed, captured and held in a prisoner-of-war camp, repatriated to Britain in 1943, and then returned to war. Eventually he was sent home when the war ended in 1945.

A few years ago a friend's husband went missing while walking in the bush in central Te Ika-a-Māui. By the time she realised he was missing it was already dark and the search party had to hold off until the morning. There was nothing my friend could do but wait for news. Was her husband simply injured in the bush? Was it something worse? To wait in this way is to understand human helplessness. With nothing to do, the mind flips between dread and optimistic self-talk, unable to find comfort in either.

My friend's husband had slipped in a river and broken his ankle in two places. He spent a wet night in a half-made tent before the search party found him the next day. My grandmother – and many women like her – spent years waiting for news. Sheila would get up in the morning, fix her hair, dress in her grey work uniform, and then catch the train, all the while uncertain where Len was or whether he would come home. I make the comparison not to downplay my friend's fear, but to find a way to imagine Sheila's.

The strongest memory I have of my grandparents is from a visit to England in the early 1980s. I was just five. My grandparents still lived in the brick family home that Mum grew up in. It had a large rambling garden flanked with apple and pear trees, and in the afternoons we'd scavenge for fruit that had fallen into the grass. I'd carry a pile of ripe fruit back to the house where, from the patio, Sheila would check on her husband as he moved slowly beneath the trees.

/

Sheila's self-responsibility and fortitude are qualities I associated not with her gender, but with her wisdom about what it meant to be human. If anything, I didn't experience my grandmother as gendered. It was rare to travel between England and Aotearoa when I was a child, so I only saw her four times while I was growing up. We became close in my twenties and thirties when we started to write letters and I could visit her as an adult. This was after she'd gone through menopause and had stopped performing the traditional signifiers of womanhood. She often dressed in slacks, a loose t-shirt and comfortable shoes. She carried a curved walnut walking stick, her grey hair cropped close to her head. When I did get to see her, I'd help her tend the garden of her retirement flat or we'd watch sport together on her boxy television. In the evenings we drank a small glass of sherry before dinner. To me, she felt genderless, fluid, ambiguous.

I'm not trying to say that Sheila didn't identify as a woman – I am sure she did – and for much of her life she performed a particular type of womanhood. After Len came back from the war and became a travelling salesman, she stayed at home to manage the household and raise their three children. I have a photograph of her smiling on a verandah in a blue summer dress, and another where she is wearing a long pleated skirt and stockings. She is short and bonny beside my tall, noble-looking grandfather. Her hair is curled under a hat and one hand is lightly looped through my grandfather's arm. When I knew her best, though, her gender did not have the same immediacy that I experience with other people. Instead, in the space where gender would have been came my grandmother's unique *personness*.

/

I don't think I can write about gender and womanhood without acknowledging gender theorist Judith Butler. Everything I read on the topic gestures to their work. Their book *Gender Trouble*, originally published in 1990, changed Western feminist theory and has been called one of the founding texts of queer theory. I found it an exhausting book to read – it's dense with jargon and seems to be written for academics. In the end, I watched a gender studies master's student explain the book on YouTube to better understand what I'd read.

In *Gender Trouble*, Butler argues that gender is not an essential and fixed quality that we are born with, but is instead *'an effect'* created by our repeated behaviours and 'stylization of the body'.[1,2] According to Butler, gender does not exist until a person's repeated behaviours 'congeal over time' into a gender identity – most commonly in Western society, as a man or a woman.[3] In short, gender isn't something we *are* but something we enact and *do*.

Even though Butler's theory of gender performativity has made its way into popular culture – often being referred to as the social construction of gender – most of us unconsciously think about gender as something that's fixed and innate, and as being linked to our biological sex. When I do a Google Dictionary search for *womanhood* it defines the term as 'the qualities considered to be natural to … a woman' where the word 'natural' implies those qualities are inborn or biological. The same entry refers me to *femininity*, which, when searched, throws up terms such as 'delicacy and prettiness' or – as Wikipedia provides – 'gentleness, empathy, humility and sensitivity'.[4]

Butler's work has sparked many necessary conversations about gender – conversations about whether some gendered traits are biologically influenced, the non-binary complexity of biological sex and how the theory of gender performativity accounts for the lived reality of trans people. Apart from the fact that I'm no expert, I feel these conversations belong to a different sort of book. While theory is an essential and important way that society moves forward, for me it operates in the lecture hall of the mind and not the soft bed of the body, which is where, eventually, change happens for all of us.

But one of Butler's ideas is of particular interest to me: that gender is something we *do*. I don't want to suggest that gender is a choice –

it isn't. I couldn't wake up tomorrow morning and decide to be another gender. Instead, it's the idea that women can work to 'resignify' or change the meaning of painful, limiting and oppressive norms.[5] I want to hold this idea up to the light. I want to take the back off the idea and tinker with its insides. What does the idea feel like held deep inside my body? Because if womanhood is not something fixed and innate, then neither are the behaviours that I've learned make up womanhood. To see gender this way gives me – and other women – the ability, to an extent, to create our own gender.

/

A few years ago, some of the women around me shaved one side of their head in an undercut while leaving the rest of their hair long. I thought it was a sexy subversion of the societal norm that women have long hair. I think Butler would have approved as the style both 'mimed and displaced', two qualities she says are necessary to subvert gender norms.[6] But the first time a friend described having her head shaved my hands leapt protectively to my own hair. My delicate, pretty, gentle, empathetic, humble and sensitive hair.

I have always had long hair – and not just any long hair, the kind that a friend enviously calls 'princess hair'. My hair would only be closer to the Western feminine ideal if it were blonde – it falls in thick chestnut waves. It has a delicate drama, like Ophelia's locks in that famous painting by John Everett Millais. Ophelia lies face up in the water, gaze skyward, wildflowers strewn around her as she drowns. And her hair, sinuous and heavy, expands like a halo.

While seeing gender as something I *do* allows me to challenge my gendered behaviours, I have found my success depends upon how entangled those behaviours are with my identity, and to what extent they give me a sense of safety. I am certainly less accommodating than I was as a younger woman. I won't let men interrupt or talk over me in conversation, and I apologise less often for things that are not my fault after I started to notice *sorry* came out of my mouth any time it could. My own voice was betraying my inner sorriness at what – my ideas, my self? Being a woman saying things?

I was glad of the company when I read that Maggie Nelson also had to unlearn her sorry habit after she noticed the word appeared in most of her work emails.[7] One year I refused to make a cake for my son's school fair. I felt that the school assumed that – as a woman – I'd know how to bake and that baking was the way I'd want to contribute. I didn't say sorry, but instead offered to do the social media. I'm learning to be okay with being seen as 'difficult' when I challenge these sorts of gender norms. Still, I can't cut my long hair. Maybe that is because my hair is always loved, even when I am not.

In terms of our public bodies, hair might be the physical attribute most laden with gender expectations. Hair was involved the first time I realised that gender was more complex than I'd been told. When I was about six or seven I stayed the night on a marae with my mum and sister. Mum was attending a hui to set up the cervical cancer screening programme in Aotearoa, and she'd brought us with her. While the grownups were speaking, my sister and I played tag with a girl in the large vaulted dining hall. She'd also been brought to the hui and was shorter than me with long brown hair. When I was 'it', I chased her around and around a dining table, each of us dodging and skidding, until I finally tagged her on the arm. 'She's it!' I yelled to my sister. The other child pulled up and grimaced. 'I'm no girl,' he said.

Even now, four decades later, I notice how firmly rooted my own gender expectations can be. Over the years Sam has gone from wearing his hair short and cropped to a style that falls to the middle of his back. He is regularly misgendered by other parents or strangers in the supermarket, all because of his long hair. But more than that, I notice that my own experience of his gender has subtly changed;

to me he feels less like a boy and more gender neutral because of his hair. Will my experience of him change again as he enters puberty and thick hair starts to cover his body? It probably will. Dark hair sprouting from a jaw line, wiry black hair curling from underneath an arm, long straight leg hair carpeting a thigh – this hair also holds gender expectations.

Reading the stories of seven non-binary people interviewed in 'Vibrant Colors, Buzzcuts, & Freedom' on *Refinery29*, I notice one theme emerges: hair is a way to step out of the gender binary and to prioritise self-acceptance over societal acceptance. As artist Katayoun discovered, though, people treated them differently depending on how they presented, and often their gender was read incorrectly. For instance, when Katayoun wore their hair long and with a fringe they were 'always coded as femme' but once they adopted a more masculine hairstyle, people assumed they were 'trans masc'.[8] Katayoun continues: 'I want to be able to experiment with how I look and not worry about how I'm read … Interactions can make you feel really wrong or really right.'[9]

Butler wrote *Gender Trouble* in part to understand gay women's experience of stepping outside of gender norms and the resulting feeling – as Katayoun calls it – of being 'wrong'. Although I imagine the feeling is persistent for people who always live outside of gender norms, women can also experience that wrongness at times. As Butler explains, to be a 'woman' is to inherently exist in a gender framework, and 'one is a woman' depending on how well she meets the expectations of the framework.[10] While each woman may have a clear sense of her own personhood, the 'stability and coherence' of her experience of womanhood can be disrupted when others misread her gender or tell her she's doing her gender incorrectly, a behaviour called gender policing.[11, 12] Quite often as a child – usually when I was at some family gathering and enthusiastically helping myself to food – I was told that my behaviour was 'not polite', which was code for unladylike. I couldn't both be a good girl and show my hunger at the same time. But I was hungry! Why couldn't I be both good and hungry? To step outside of gender norms was to feel dislocated from my own body.

A failure to meet gender norms leads to more severe outcomes than being scolded at the dinner table. When Indian-British writer Sharan Dhaliwal cut her hair short it changed her social standing. In Dhaliwal's community long hair signified 'being chaste, marriage material, whereas short or shaved hair related to promiscuity and shame'.[13] 'No one's going to marry you now', her mother told her.[14] 'I really didn't have a deep understanding of how optics affected my personal identity', Dhaliwal says of the experience.[15]

And more severe? American civil rights organisation Human Rights Campaign reported that at least forty-seven transgender women and gender non-conforming people were killed in hate crimes in the United States in 2018 and 2019, with the victims being disproportionately women of colour.[16] In October 2020, they reported that 'at least 44 transgender or gender non-conforming people' had been killed in hate crimes, with the majority being Black and Latinx transgender women.[17] Such violent transphobia stems from narrow gender norms and the repression they create. As gender non-conforming writer and performer Alok Vaid-Menon states: '[It's] a system that rewards conformity and not creativity … Repression breeds insecurity breeds violence.'[18]

Everything from chastisement to violence aims to keep women's behaviour locked within gender norms, and the stories I've heard show me that gender policing happens in all parts of a woman's life. In her TED talk 'I don't want children – stop telling me I'll change my mind', essayist Christen Reighter describes her decision to live childfree and the impossibility of getting elective sterilisation surgery.[19] Even though she met the legal requirements, doctors refused to give her the surgery because being childfree did not fit with their idea of womanhood. Reighter reports other women had similar experiences when seeking sterilisation – women without children were told to come back once they had a child, whereas women with children were told to have more. One doctor suggested to Reighter that a future partner might want children, with the implication being that this imaginary partner's needs should override her own.

Reighter felt disheartened and angry. 'I've always believed that having children was an extension of womanhood, not the definition … that strips [a woman] of her entire identity as an adult unto herself', she says.[20] She continues: 'It's so easy to forget the roles that society places on us are more than mere titles. What about the weight that comes with them, the pressure to conform to these standards … the fear associated with questioning them, and the desires we cast aside to accept them?'[21] After years of persistence, Reighter finally convinced a surgeon to do the procedure.

What I find inspiring about Reighter's story is the way she did not internalise her desire to be childfree as a failure of her womanhood. To externalise that negativity – to not locate the problem in ourselves – is to inhabit womanhood in expansive and self-compassionate ways. It is the process through which women have expanded and changed the norms of womanhood. As Butler says, our task is 'not whether to repeat, but how to repeat or, indeed, to repeat and, through a radical proliferation of gender, to *displace* the very gender norms that enable the repetition itself'.[22] In other words, to make gender trouble.

/

To return to my grandmother, to say I experienced her as genderless is really to say that she wasn't performing the behaviours that I associated with womanhood. My comment shows the limitations of how I understood gender at the time, rather than anything true about Sheila.

While the origin of my expectations can't be reduced to a single moment, a few stand out. I remember the crushed-velvet dress I wore to a school ball when I was fourteen. It was a maroon, off-the-shoulder number that I'd hired from a bridal shop. They'd had very few options that were not white, and while the dress fitted through my hips, it clenched my ribcage and chest. My mum reached into the back of her closet and handed me a pair of black suede heels. They were slightly too large, but my feet looked like sleek sea creatures swimming across the blue carpet. I stood in front of the bedroom mirror, a girl swallowed in ruching.

While nothing quite fitted, I liked what I saw. My hair was curled and I had lipstick on. I thought I looked a little like Julia Roberts in *Pretty Woman* after she's made over by Héctor Elizondo as the hotel manager. My wildness had been smoothed out. Like Roberts' character Vivian, I suddenly felt acceptable: a proper woman. When my date arrived he pinned an oversized corsage to the neckline of my dress. 'You look so pretty!' he said. He was only fifteen, his smooth cheeks flushed pink, his rented tuxedo jacket too long on his arms. I had the sense that we were playing grownups; we were seeing how adultness fit. We sat in the kitchen while my parents took photos, his arm stiff around my bare shoulders, my hands clasped neatly on my lap.

Taking off the expectations of womanhood has been like taking off that suffocating dress. I expand with space and air. I've started tramping again, something I haven't done since childhood. Recently, while staying in a tramping hut on a quick overnight trip, my friend Leslie and I needed kindling to light a fire. It was early spring and we were high enough in the Ruahine Ranges for snow to still be on the ground. Our breath fogged in the air as we followed a short track up the hill to the woodshed. We turned towards the view. Beyond our hut's roofline, the misty green expanse of the Manawatū stretched to the horizon. A far-off mountain a smudge in the distance. Lying in the grass beside the woodshed was a steel axe, the handle connected by a chain to the wall so opportunistic hikers didn't take it with them. Why anyone would have carried it out I don't know – it was heavy and the head, corroded from years of alpine weather, was blunt.

Leslie and I gathered quarter moons of wood from the musty shed and stood them up on the cutting block, their ringed faces flat to the sky. I heaved the axe behind my shoulder. The muscles in my thighs stood in relief, my feet were spread apart for balance, my teeth bared. I curved the axe down and smashed it through the first piece of wood. I know these details because Leslie, laughing at the sight, took a photograph. She wasn't laughing because I looked ridiculous – although I probably did – but from the surprise and ecstatic joy that had risen up between us, away from our families and domestic worlds, churning up the mud with our feet.

On that tramp I took *Flash Count Diary* by Darcey Steinke – a beautiful memoir that explores Steinke's experience of menopause, a phase I am entering. I read it at night by the light of my head torch, my body enfolded by my sleeping bag. What intrigued me most about Steinke's story was the way she found midlife and menopause began an 'ungendering' process.[23] I wondered if this would happen to me too. While the hormonal changes of menopause meant she lost female signifiers such as smooth skin and shiny hair, Steinke also stopped performing acts of traditional womanhood – she began to dress in androgynous clothing and to go without makeup. Although Steinke grieves for her younger self, she finds the transformation lets her step outside the 'brutal binary' of masculinity and femininity.[24] She starts to experience 'a wider emotional sweep, a larger sense of the world, and a keener awareness' of herself.[25]

While writing *Flash Count Diary*, Steinke researches post-reproductive animals to make sense of the way ungendering makes her feel animalistic. Of all of the animals Steinke reads about, she becomes obsessed with matriarch orca whales, who along with humans are one of the few animals to go through menopause. She fixates on Lolita, a post-reproductive orca whale who has lived at the Miami Seaquarium since 1970. Lolita was captured on the northern border of Puget Sound – a system of waterways near Seattle, Washington, which are part of the Salish Sea. She was one of a group of whales that were herded by boats and explosives into a net, and is the only surviving whale from the capture. The tank she lives in at the Miami Seaquarium is the smallest orca enclosure in North America, spanning only four times her body length. Whales in captivity like Lolita often swim repeatedly into the concrete walls of their tank, smashing their skulls until they are dead.

In the hut that night, I read the chapter where Steinke flies to Miami to see Lolita for the first time. She joins the animal rights protesters outside the aquarium who are calling for Lolita's release, but she wants to get closer to the giant animal. Steinke buys a ticket to Lolita's show and is mesmerised as the whale does tricks for the audience – she plunges down before launching her entire body above the water. The performance is impressive, but it is Lolita's captivity that Steinke relates to and thinks about the most. She says,

> *I recognize the feeling of being held captive, not literally, like Lolita, but metaphorically. A female captivity always binding but that, without fertility, tightens further. I am restricted, stuck in the box the greater culture uses to enclose and reduce older women.*[26]

After seeing Lolita, Steinke takes a kayak trip on the Salish Sea, where she hopes to catch sight of Granny or J2 – an orca matriarch born in 1911. In the wild, matriarchs like Granny lead their family groups, teach younger whales the hunting grounds, pod rituals and vocalisations, and take care of young while their mothers forage for food. They also train younger whales in sexual techniques. Granny leads not only her own pod, but two other pods in the Salish Sea. I can tell that while Steinke sees Lolita as symbolising womanhood's captivity, Granny symbolises the freedom that can come from menopause.

It's nearly midnight when I read the next passage. Everyone else is asleep in the hut so I've shimmied down into the sleeping bag until it folds over the top of my head. I hold the book in a halo of light. Steinke joins a kayak group at Smallpox Bay. They practise kayak techniques – the 'straddle-butt drop, and side-swing in' – then the group paddles out into the water.[27] Around them are fried-egg jellyfish and floating beds of bull kelp. As the kayaks clear the mouth of the bay, one of the group calls out. He's seen a whale in the distance. The group rafts up and grips each other's paddles to draw the kayaks together – the wash from the whales could tip them over. Talking stops. The whales swim toward them, their dorsal fins high in the air. As the sea surges, Granny breaks the surface alongside Steinke – '*Kawouf!*' Granny's brown eye looks directly at her.[28]

After seeing Granny, Steinke tries to make sense of her experience: 'I felt a little as I had the night after my daughter was born. After pushing out a creature wet with saltwater and blood … Seeing J2 was like having my daughter, an event outside human evaluation.'[29] On the phone to a friend she describes seeing Granny, but feels her words reduce the experience. 'What I felt was a dilation,' she writes.[30]

/

On the day I return from my Ruahine tramp I sit in the shower and let the hot water rush over me. I think about Steinke and Butler and try to experience my body as ungendered, an animal. My legs ache from the tramp. I squeeze them gently. They are functional and useful. I see the folds of my stomach, my breasts uneven from breastfeeding, the loose pouches of flesh on my inner thighs. Fine-haired and tubular, I remind myself of the naked mole rat Sam and I once googled.

I think about when I used to go tramping as a child. Being in the mountains was one of the few times I could escape the expectations of good girlhood. When climbing I could be assertive and pick out my own route. It was okay to be hungry because I'd earned it. And although I often felt cold and exhausted, I instinctively knew how to be in my body. When descending a rock scree I'd lean back and dig in my heels. I knew how to avoid thorny matagouri bushes and to step over rabbit holes. I felt so sure in the capabilities of my body that when my father organised a group of men to climb Ben McLeod – a peak that is part of the Te Waipounamu sheep station of the same name – I fumed at them that tramping was 'not only for boys'.

It took five hours that day to scale Ben McLeod, the dots of our bodies etching the side. As we reached the summit, the sun touched the far valley below and the distant peaks turned luminous. The braided Rangitata River spread out before us. Hot and vibrant, I flew down the descent. As a child I was light and agile, so I soon found myself ahead of the group. When I reached the lower slopes, a hare darted along the fence line and paused, ears upright. I held my body still. The hare looked at me and I looked at the hare. For a second, I felt the hare's *thereness* and then it was gone, into the scrub. Of wonder, Buddhist practitioner Kittisaro says: 'One starts to get a sense of being part of something vast'.[31]

Steinke's description of becoming ungendered reminds me of being on the side of the mountain and of the presence of my grandmother. Like Steinke's 'dilation' it's an expansive feeling: an addition rather than a subtraction. It's a spaciousness I'm starting to find in myself. Steinke's daughter sums it up well after Steinke suggests there should be many more genders: 'You don't get it,' she says. 'Each person is their own gender. There are as many genders as there are human beings.'[32]

/

Just before my forty-second birthday I tramp with three friends to Waitewaewae Hut, a sixteen-bunk Department of Conservation hut on the bank of the Ōtaki River. We leave early on a Saturday morning, driving out of Te Whanganui-a-Tara and up the Kāpiti Coast. The island glitters in the morning light. We turn inland toward the Tararua Ranges and wind our way along a narrow road until we reach the Ōtaki Forks campsite, our starting point for the tramp. Lush bush grows above us.

In the carpark, we adjust our bags and then prop one of our cellphones up on the car. We take a pre-tramp photograph: four women, ready. I stand on the right, my sunglasses pushed back on my head. Kristina stands beside me, swamped in a grey waterproof jacket. She's a head shorter than me and later will earn the nickname 'mountain goat' for the way she effortlessly springs between boulders. Next to her Rhiannon has been caught mid-laugh, her face bright and open in the morning sun. On the far side stands Kirsten, orange jacket zipped up to her chin, her blond hair haloed under a cap.

From the carpark we cross a swing bridge and climb up to an exposed river terrace. Huge slips have gouged out the hillside, so we follow a new track that detours around them. We stop on the edge of one slip and marvel at where the earth has fallen away, the green face of the hill now exposed dirt. We feel a little dangerous, as though we're engaging in something taboo. In a way we are: to be absent from our families and duties is to be selfish. And women aren't selfish.

Soon we turn into dense bush and the track disappears. Branches float above us like ghostly limbs. We navigate using triangular orange trail markers that are nailed to trees. Sometimes we go for minutes without seeing a marker – the group stopping to scan the bush, unsure if we've gone the wrong way – then someone spots an orange flash among the green.

Our progress is hard and slow. The track works its way between knotted trees, roots curled up like snares, the ground uneven and slippery. At times it's so steep that we climb on our hands and knees, one woman after another. We reach down and pull each other up. We shout encouragement. My thighs and shoulders start to burn under the weight of my pack and my legs are caked with mud. Thin red scratches appear across my thighs. I grunt and huff as I climb. Maybe this is why tramping didn't survive my passage from girlhood to womanhood: to tramp is to be unlovely.

After four hours we reach the halfway point – a forest plateau turned bog – and perch on tree roots to eat our lunch. Rhi breaks up a block of chocolate and Kirsten hands around her gummy snakes. We've found the immediate camaraderie that I only experience with other women. The air is damp and sweet. Long stems of moss dangle wetly from the limbs of trees. Occasionally a bird calls, and in the distance I can hear the tumbling rush of a stream. Most of the time we eat in silence – the bush takes us into itself. I lie back. My body sinks into the soft ground as though I've always been here.

Eventually we descend along a roaring stream and pop out onto the banks of the Ōtaki River. A cheer goes up. We've walked for seven hours and the hut is moments away. To make it to the hut, we have to enter the river, cross to the far side where the water is shallow, wade fifty metres downstream, and then cross back to the bank we've just come from. The route will bypass the deep and dangerous parts of the river and the inaccessible cliffs that run down its edge.

As a child I'd crossed rivers with my family, but I'd never attempted it as an adult. We survey the river and decide to enter on a wide bend. Although the water is swift, it only reaches our knees. We unclip our chest straps, link arms, and step into the water. Edging out, we turn against the current. It pulls at my feet and calves. My boots are immediately saturated and my toes burn with the cold. Unsteady on the slick rocks, we roll and bump our bodies together. 'Keep going,' someone shouts, and we clasp each other until our eight-legged animal reaches the shallows. Here the water is slow and slippery, but we easily wade downstream. For a moment, I pause and look up. The mountains are huge above me. The sky unfurls vast and white. They enter my chest and I feel my heart beating with them. 'Sarah, are you ready?' asks Kristina. We cross.

/

Sometimes I think womanhood is a place in which I'm lost. A place that I'm trying to walk my way out of. Months after the tramp, in our group chat, Kirsten says that being in the bush made her feel as though she'd stepped out of regular time and experienced time the way trees might. Kristina said that the tramp had brought her back to her body after 'eight years in the parental wilderness'. I also felt changed by the trip. I had discovered that being unlovely in the company of other women helped me understand my womanhood. It made me think of a line from Steinke's book: 'Since I've stopped my struggle to be beautiful, I am overtaken by beauty more often.'[33]

To be dirty. To be tired and rough, outspoken and selfish and hungry. That is to be a woman. That is to be human. When I was younger becoming a woman meant – in many small cuts – abandoning parts of myself. Now I'm taking them back and abandoning the parts that don't fit.

Chapter Four
Genealogy of care

After writing the first few chapters of this book I thought I would never get it finished. I couldn't find the time. I was working as a writer for a charity that provides computer programming lessons to kids. It was interesting and reasonably paid work, but by the time I'd finished my hours and then chores around the house, it was time to drive down the hill and pick up Sam from school. He'd often bring a friend home and I found it difficult to write with kids in the house. Their squeals and crashing, although mostly joyous, fragmented my attention. There was also afternoon tea to make and questions to be answered. *What's the largest number with a name? Where's the Sellotape? Can we have a biscuit?*

When it was just Sam at home I felt the pull of his wanting. He'd fidget with boredom. He'd mope around the lounge and flop down on the couch. He would come into our 'study', the tiny third bedroom where Sam and I each have a desk and which also houses our kitchen pantry. He'd slink his body on to my lap, his skinny arms looped around my neck. 'Mummy', he'd say. The incantation nearly always worked.

Our late afternoons would gallop into evening and the ritual of dinner, shower and bed. I've always found something precious about this time of night, when the work of the day is done. Although nearly ten, Sam turns giddy and unselfconscious. He dances in jerky movements around the lounge or sings a poor imitation of opera, his mouth open wide and one hand outstretched to an imagined audience. It's as if, with the full attention of both his parents, he also becomes full. I wouldn't give up this time in the evening for anything, not even to write.

One morning I sat in our study and tried to work out a schedule that would mean I could finish the book. Jim takes Sam to school around 8.30am, so as soon as the house was empty, I reasoned, I could sit at our old dining table and start a timer. I'd write for twenty-five minutes before taking a short break, during which I would stack the dishwasher or hang out the washing, or do whatever other chore needed to be done. I'd repeat this pattern of writing and chores for two hours, and only then would I begin my paid work. I noted down the days that I run and the one afternoon I volunteer. If I was really strict, I could get everything done. I wrote the schedule out in a notebook: Monday to Sunday down the red-ruled margin of the page, the times and tasks of each day spidering out.

The act felt so familiar that I went back and looked through my old notebooks and found similar schedules. Some were from only six months ago. Another was from last year. Many were from when Sam was a toddler. I went down into our basement and hauled out the blue plastic bin that I use to store old papers and keepsakes. I squatted down and pried off the lid. Underneath a chess set and a pile of old university essays, I found some yellowed notebooks that I've kept from my twenties and thirties. I opened them. Monday to Sunday down the margin of the page. Times and tasks. It was like finding an archaeological record of the way I've controlled and pushed myself over the years. Of the way I believe that writing something down can make it possible.

/

I didn't intend to become the primary carer for Sam. I'd assumed, naively as it turns out, that after having a baby Jim and I would both work part-time and split the parenting. That even though our lives would be fuller and it would be harder, I'd have time to write. When I was pregnant, and for the first two years of Sam's life, I was finishing a creative writing doctorate in poetry and teaching creative writing online, both at Massey University. Most of my income came from my doctoral scholarship, which had no paid maternity leave. Jim only had two weeks' paternity leave. We'd just bought our first home, a tiny 1959 bungalow in Te Whanganui-a-Tara with a steeply sloped garden, and we didn't have a lot of money. As I was the one already working from home it made sense – along with the mess of breastfeeding and weeks of bleeding after childbirth – that I would be the one to be home with Sam. And the love story between me and my son was just beginning. I ached to be home with him, but also it was easiest. In those blurry, tired years we often went with what was easiest.

When Sam was nearly a year old, he started going to daycare each morning. We'd been lucky to get him into a daycare close to our home. At 8am, I'd place him in the arms of his cheerful carer, drive the five minutes back home and work on my doctorate for a couple of hours. At 10am I'd drive back to the daycare to feed him, my breasts sore and leaking by the time I arrived. Some days I would lie down beside him in the sleep room until he slept, a soft blanket tucked over his body, his pale cheeks glowing in the dark. I wanted to sleep too, but instead I'd drive home and do some teaching work before I picked him up at midday. We'd spend the afternoon together on the local swings or building fantastical worlds with his toys at home. While he was still young enough for afternoon naps, I'd work through them. In a photo from this time I am cradling him in one arm, his face smooth and flushed with sleep, while I type on my laptop with the other hand. This is how I wrote my doctorate.

Around the time he turned three I started to have dizzy spells. If I stood up too quickly the world would drop away. Sometimes the sick spinning feeling came on when I was seated. I remember sitting in a café near his daycare, my laptop open in front of me, when my vision started to prickle black at the edges. The sound of people talking became muffled and distant as though I had plunged into water. A sour taste came into my mouth. I put my forehead down on the café table, eyes closed, and willed the world to come back. It must have looked to other people as though I were sleeping or praying. In a way I was. *Hold on*, I said to myself. After doing a panel of blood tests my doctor, a kind man with jumpy energy, told me that all the results were normal and that what I was experiencing was simply exhaustion. 'It's just parenthood,' he said with a wry laugh. Had I thought about getting some more rest?

After I finished my doctorate I received funding to turn my thesis into a collection of long poems. This would be my second collection and I was grateful and relieved that it would be in the world. The funding wasn't enough to cover my portion of the family income, but it meant I could drop one of the university courses I was teaching. It took seven months to write the book, and by the time I'd finished – I remember summer was beginning in a humid pulse of heat and long days – Sam was four and a half. My baby had become a pre-schooler. I'd been working from home and being his primary carer for nearly five years. Soon he would start school, and I had the sense of surfacing – of rising up out of the gloom and weeds and muck – to draw a breath.

When I think back to those early years of motherhood I remember how frayed and paper-thin I felt. The smallest thing upset me. Walking to the shops one afternoon, not long after finishing the poetry collection, I fell in step behind a young woman with a stroller. It was a warm clear day with only a wisp of cloud in the sky. She had bouncy blonde hair that shimmered in the sunlight. After a few minutes her toddler started to cry. The child's low wail came in little punches of sound. Wail. Stop. Wail. The young woman did nothing. She didn't stoop down or make any comforting noises. She didn't hand the child a toy or some food. After five minutes of listening to the child's mournful cries, I found myself – to later shame – shouting at her. 'Take care of your baby!' I yelled, coming right up to her. She recoiled from me, her eyes wide. 'It's her hunger cry. She's just hungry,' she said. I marched away from her, back up the hill. I knew the baby was okay. I knew, in some calmer part of myself, that I was angry at this young woman for giving herself a break. It was something I hadn't been able to give to myself and I could no longer swallow down the hurt.

And on occasion, I had started to hurt myself. On the worst days, I would climb into a hot shower and slide down into its plastic well. I was hollow with tiredness. The rush of water covered my wail-crying, or at least I hoped it did. Sometimes Sam's tiny face ghosted a query across the shower door. 'I'm just tired,' I'd say in a high cheerful tone. He'd wander off, his trust in me making everything all right. Curled in the shower I felt desperate to push the shame out of me. *I knew women who worked more hours than I did and who had more children. They seemed okay – why wasn't I?* These thoughts looped and grew and cut until my body ballooned into panic and I punched myself hard on the top of my skull – that's where people wouldn't see the bruises. After I'd punched the terror out of me, I'd turn off the water. I'd dry my body, pull on my clothes and keep going.

Around the same time, Holly Walker published a book called
The Whole Intimate Mess about her experience of being an MP while
raising her daughter Esther. She writes:

> *I'm on the floor, raining blows on the side of my own head, and
> then smashing it into the ground. I'm screaming, crawling up
> the hallway, sobbing. I've lost hold of my tenuous grip on myself,
> become something wild, animal … Some days, it felt like we were
> making it work. But right under the surface, not very far down,
> was the crazy person who could punch herself in the face.*[1]

When I read Walker's story I was not surprised. I also felt like
something wild and animal, and as though I could turn on myself at
any time.

/

What I hadn't realised about being Sam's primary carer was that I
would slowly and imperceptibly become responsible for my family's
care work until it was nearly all mine. I was the person to take Sam
to the doctor and go to his school plays. I organised permission slips
and playdates; haircuts and fingernail trimming; school books and
pencil cases; new clothes and shoes and togs and regulation sunhats
and birthday presents and Christmas presents and presents for his
friends' birthdays; holiday programmes and sports enrolments and
the six beautiful and complex weeks of the summer holidays that
annual leave never quite covers; lunch boxes and Monday dinner and
Tuesday dinner and most other dinners, after which I'd teach him
how to wash his little body and comb his hair and how to unload
a dishwasher and how to say sorry and how to speak up and how
to write a thank you note, and that the other person's address goes
on the front, and yours goes on the back, and the stamp goes in the
corner and then how to slide it into the post box. I wanted to do all of
these things, but I didn't want to be the only one.

Novelist Lynn Steger Strong writes, 'There is nothing more sustaining to long-term creative work than time and space – and these things cost money'.[2] The reason Jim wasn't there to help me was because he was working full-time and earning most of our family's income. We didn't want much: a child, a small house of our own, a few books. Reading Strong's words it occurs to me that if society valued and supported the arts in a fuller way, then I wouldn't need two jobs – one that earns money and one that produces creative work. It also occurs to me that the same can be said for parenting and care work – my third job. What is not sustaining for creative imagining is fitting it into small pockets of time in a life where you're already exhausted.

That is what I see other women who are writers do, especially those who have children. I try not to compare myself to them when I see their posts on social media. One friend gets up at 5am to write before heading off to a full day of work. Another posts that she writes six days a week – only Sunday for a rest! Another writes books while home schooling and also working her day job. As their posts scroll into my feed I shrink away in shame. To be honest, I've started to mute them.

I can no longer work in that way. I tore the new schedule out of my notebook and threw it in the bin – an act of protest. And a self-compassionate part of me wonders if these women are also doing violence to themselves. If, after they wake in the dark, the coffee slowly boiling on the stove, they feel their world spin.

/

A few years ago I read *Past Caring? Women, work and emotion*, a selected history of women's care work in Aotearoa, and found that the way my family divides up care work is not by accident. The book explores the 'shadow labour' on which Aotearoa was built, and the way care work, both paid and unpaid, continues to fall to women.[3] Though essential for society, care work is 'often invisible, usually accorded little value and only sometimes recognized as skilled.'[4]

In *Past Caring?* historian Barbara Brookes notes that '[i]n the last decades of the twentieth century, women's participation in the labour force increased at double the rate of men's', but that women's care work did not decrease.[5] Instead, women have to fit paid employment around their care work. Prue Hyman comes to the same conclusion in her book *Hopes Dashed? The economics of gender inequality.* Hyman cites figures from a Statistics New Zealand 1998–99 time use survey, which found:

> Women on average did two hours more unpaid work a day than men (4.8 compared with 2.8) and two hours less paid work a day (16 weekly, compared with 29). But women with young children who are also in paid work had the longest weeks of all, and women did 64 per cent of all the unpaid work, 87 per cent of which was in the household.[6]

The reason for the imbalance is that women have joined a workforce modelled on the traditional male working week. The patriarchal model assumes much: that men will have a woman at home to do their care work for them; that men do not want to do care work or support dependants (except financially); that relationships are heteronormative; and that families are two-parent households.

While the model is particularly detrimental to women, I've also found it doesn't support men to be partners who equally share the domestic care. In the early years of Sam's life, Jim tried to negotiate part-time work with his employers, only to be told that it wasn't possible. He works in the tech sector, a notoriously male-dominated industry, and he often found himself in conversation with a male boss whose woman partner was at home caring for their children. Jim came away from these failed negotiations feeling frustrated.

The subtext was that, as a man, his priority should be work over family life. Recently a friend's husband took a day off work to care for their sick toddler. His employers – a public sector organisation – were put out. Why wasn't his wife the one to take the day off? How outrageous that a man should want to care for his child! As Brookes succinctly summarises, 'traditionally, to be considered a "good woman" meant putting others first; to be a "good man" was to put work first'.[7]

Reading Brookes and Hyman, I start to see how the traditional male working week doesn't acknowledge the way society's economy *relies* on care work. Since having a child, Jim's ability to be in paid work has been *directly* related to my caring for Sam. The amount he has cared for Sam has also *directly* impacted my career and income. Before we had a child Jim and I earned roughly the same salary. We were both working in IT at the time, him as an engineer and me writing process and strategy. Eight years after having Sam, Jim's yearly bonus was more than my *entire* yearly income. '[I]t is important also to remember [unpaid work's] interdependence with paid work,' writes Hyman, and '[t]he disproportionate amount of unpaid caring work that women do affects their outcomes in the paid labour market'.[8] Even though the government funds twenty hours of early childhood education per week for children aged three and over (and after that public schooling), that is only a small proportion of childhood. 'What would happen if caregivers withdrew their labour?' Brookes asks. 'How many children would be wandering the streets?'[9]

For previous generations, caring for dependants was the responsibility of family or was taken on by a 'benevolent or church institution'.[10] Now, families with sufficient income can employ commercial care to cover the shortfall, not only for childcare but for care of our elderly family members as well. Brookes' own life is an example of how women use commercial care. She writes:

My own career has been made possible by that very context:
my children were all in daycare from infancy, in after-school
care at primary school, and my mother spent her last years
in a small rest home near our house. My academic work
took priority over caring in a way that would have been
unimaginable in my mother's life.[11]

The problem with outsourcing care work is that it doesn't change the systemic issue of how care work is valued. Also, the people providing commercial care work, such as early-childhood teachers and rest-home carers, are disproportionately women, and '[b]ecause caring work is done by women, it is underpaid'.[12] A 2012 Human Rights Commission report into the aged-care workforce found that the '[m]aintenance men and gardeners at residential facilities are routinely paid more than the women who do arduous daily tasks assisting residents'.[13]

Women who work in commercial care often have families of their own, but – because they are working – are unavailable to care for their dependants. Due to low wages they may also be unable to afford commercial care for their families, or be able to access only poor-quality care, or have to place their children in care very early and for extensive periods (a combination that poses the greatest risk to a child's psychological and cognitive development).[14,15] Paying for commercial care does not address the issue of the way care is valued and undertaken by society – it simply means it's no longer your issue.

/

I grew up learning that care work was done by women. Even though my parents both worked full-time in demanding academic positions, I never in my entire childhood saw my father cook the family dinner. My mum always did the cooking. She was the parent to bandage us when we gashed open a leg or scraped an arm. She was, and still is, the one who listened to our worries. She took on the mental and emotional load of daily family life.

As a child, I noticed the women around me liked to please people and call it care. As a teenager I was told to smile because my moods, normal and hormonal, made others uncomfortable. I needed to greet visitors who came to the house even when I desperately wanted to stay in my room – to 'present myself for inspection', as my mother called it. 'What a polite young lady,' colleagues of my parents would say.

From when I was little, I learned that other people's feelings deserved more care than my own. I can see this clearly in my first memory. I'm three. My father and I are leaving their office at Canterbury University. We walk down the hall and into the old elevator, which clanks and grinds and then gently descends. A few moments later we shudder to a stop and the doors slide open. We're stuck between two floors. I can see the skeleton of the building, the layers of carpet, metal and concrete. The lights in the elevator flicker, and my father, in a single movement, sweeps up my body and pushes me through the gap between elevator and floor. Dad clambers out after me. Years later when I wrote out this memory in a therapy exercise, I was surprised by what I found. Instead of fear, I was worried about my father's feelings – how could I make them okay?

The games my friends and I played as children were games of care. Although I didn't have one, I remember a friend playing with a Baby Alive doll as I enviously looked on. The baby wore a bib and a floral dress, her plastic mouth frozen open. My friend spooned pink liquid into the doll's mouth and then fed her with a miniature bottle. *You're such a good girl*, she'd say. Once the 'food' came out a hole in the bottom of the doll, my friend changed her nappy. Then the baby was ready for her next meal, and the care game began again.

As we grew older there were other ways to play at care. Along with miniature kitchens and tea sets there was Barbie and her short pink dresses, fake cosmetics and princess costumes – toys that taught us to be passive and beautiful while caring, because being pretty is a form of care.[16] That care play has now gone virtual. The computer game *The Sims,* which involves caring for a virtual community of people, has a majority of women players.[17]

My own care play came in many forms, such as bandaging my soft toy turtle when he got 'injured' (most of the toys that I cared for were male). If another child felt unwell, I would get them to lie down on the couch and place the back of my hand on their forehead to mimic the way my mum cared for me. I also had a toy farmyard set and I would spend hours caring for the animals. I spread the set out on our psychedelic red-and-black 60s carpet and clipped together the plastic fences to make pens and fields. The tiny sheep and chickens were placed inside, grouped into families, and then I stood plastic trees along the fence line. I thought the animals would like the green shade. Once the farm was complete, I would take the plastic woman in her black smock and white apron and feed the animals. She'd lean over the fence as the animals crowded around. In one hand she held a bucket of feed, her other hand forever outstretched.

My identity as a carer, with all the gender baggage it carries, has been hard to separate from my womanhood: the two feel twined together. That is because, as historian Jane McCabe writes, 'All caring occurs at the endpoint of a genealogy of care, moving through families and cultures, and across shifting social contexts.'[18] My caring has deep ancestral roots. And even though I know society constructs women as carers – I wasn't born wanting to clean dishes or to make a bed – care work brings me the most joy and connection with others.

A few months ago Sam had his first real injury. Jim was refurbishing a coffee machine and had hung its metal skin on the washing line to dry after spray-painting it an electric blue. Sam raced across our lawn and caught his head on the skin's sharp corner. The moment I heard his frightened cry, I knew *something* had happened. I looked out the window and saw him kneeling on the ground, blood bright across his face. When I reached him, he was clutching his forehead and crying. He lifted his hand and revealed a pulsing gash above his eye. I scooped him up and carried him back into the house. Jim ran to get a wet facecloth and I held it against the wound. Sam was sobbing. 'I'm scared,' he kept on saying. 'I'm scared.' I was scared too but I held him in my lap, rocking gently. 'I know,' I said, 'but I've got you. I'll take care of you. I've got you.'

The gash, though a bleeder, wasn't serious. We took a trip to Wellington Hospital where a nurse glued the cut together. By the time his wound was dressed (and with a lemonade ice block in hand) Sam felt safe again. That day, caring for him was all that I wanted. I know his experience of feeling safe and loved – in that moment, and in his broader life – flowers from the care that Jim and I give. I know that society rewards me for my devotion to care with a psychological safety reserved especially for women – a caring woman is loveable and acceptable and does not risk being seen as selfish or difficult. But I have strong friendships because of shared care. I have a strong marriage because of care. I volunteer and donate and compost because I believe in care. Care is good.

But the care I value is given freely. It is not care expected from me because I am a woman, while others are let off the hook. Jim and I are standing on our front doorstep. It's early morning and he's trying to leave for work, but I am upset. His face looks pained – sort of sorry, a little wary. 'Why'd you put them in the dryer?' I say. I hold up two shrunken socks.

Every year Mum buys Sam two pairs of merino socks from a fancy sock store. It's a ritual we've been doing since he was a toddler. Sam and I look at pictures of socks on the store's website. This year there are socks with crosses and moons, rainbow-striped socks and polka-dot socks. He chooses some turquoise socks with a moon pattern.

I email Mum the details of the socks and she orders them online. When they arrive a few days later I cut off the tags and give them a wash. When Sam gets home from school, I take a photo of him with the socks. He holds up a pair in each hand, his face an extravagant mime of surprise. We text the photo to Mum: 'Thank you!'

When we first had Sam neither Jim nor I knew anything about baby clothes, nappies, strollers or merino socks. I remember one stressful day shortly after Sam was born when I couldn't figure out how to collapse the stroller (it took ten minutes on Oriental Parade before I got it into the boot of the car). But the division of care work in a family influences the skills and knowledge each person acquires. As Sam's main carer I've learned while caring for him. I've become skilled and knowledgeable in his needs. I know which socks Mum buys for him – the brand, the process, the way it helps him learn to show gratitude. I know every part of Sam's life in this detail. Jim hasn't had the same opportunity. And repeating these tasks year on year means I've internalised that I am the one responsible for this care work in a way that Jim hasn't.

In the wonderful comic 'You Should've Asked', French artist Emma shows how women in heteronormative couples are expected to be responsible for the 'mental load' – a term used by feminists to mean remembering and organising the tasks needed to run a household. The comic shows a woman trying to feed her children, cook dinner and cater to a guest, all while her male partner sits on the couch. When a pot boils over on the stove her partner exclaims, 'But … you should've asked! I would've helped!'[19]

'When a man expects his partner to ask him to do things, he's viewing her as the manager of household chores,' the narrator explains.[20] In the comic an arrow swoops towards a frazzled woman with the label '"Household Management" Project Leader'. Underneath, a man standing with his arms casually crossed is labelled 'Underling'. I recognise these figures from my own relationship. Shouldering the mental load of being the 'manager' is another way that I take on care work. While Emma's comic describes the dynamic as one between a couple, I've also experienced it in the workplace. Once, when working as the only woman in an all-male IT team, I was asked to buy my own leaving flowers and card by my boss; he didn't consider 'that kind of thing' to be the work of my male co-workers.

Standing on the doorstep I start to cry. I explain to Jim that merino will shrink if you put it in the dryer. I say that these are the special 'Grandma socks' – we can't afford to buy them ourselves. 'I showed you them when they arrived in the post,' I say. Jim looks confused and his mouth turns down at the corners. Sam ranges around on the deck behind him, swinging his school bag. It arcs high into the air above his head. 'We've talked about this before,' I say. I know my tone is frustrated. 'Look, I'm sorry,' he says, starting to get angry. He thinks this conversation is about socks. There are bags under his eyes and his hair is sticking up on one side. He's tired, too. 'I just don't think both of us need to know about his socks,' he says.

Jim immediately realises he's made a mistake. 'What the fuck!' I yell. Sam freezes at the swear word. 'Is this what my life will be about?' I say. 'Socks!' I've started to properly cry, my hands cupping my forehead. 'Look, we need to go,' Jim says. He puts one hand on my shoulder. 'I didn't even know he had new socks,' he says.

As psychologist Jim Loehr states: 'Your life is what you agree to attend to.'[21]

/

Later, as I leave to pick up Sam from school, I see the hydrangeas are flowering. Some years ago I cleared the bank to one side of our house and planted it out. The young hydrangeas flared stubby and green against the new earth. Each autumn since, I've cut the plants back to help them bush with the next season's growth. I take the branches at their topmost bud and clip them away. Now the bank is a mass of bushes and blooms.

When I first planted the bushes I did some research online and learned that hydrangeas flower in different colours depending on soil acidity. Ours bloom crimson, sky blue and lavender. When I walk down our steps on a summer evening the colour is extravagant against the native garden. I've always liked hydrangeas for their jewel colours but also for the way they fade to something piebald and muddy. It seems to me a stand against beauty – or a stand for another kind of beauty.

I've been on the phone to my friend Kirsten. I told her about the socks and how everything feels too much. Jim and I have already made up. *You're right. I'm sorry*, came a text an hour after we argued. *It's not your fault*, I replied, because it isn't. To say he hasn't internalised responsibility for our family's care work is easily flipped to say that I've internalised it too much. We're both part of a system that coerces us to play roles based on gender.

Still, I'm feeling down and a bit desperate. 'I don't think I'm going to be able to write this book,' I say to Kirsten, who is also a writer. 'Why don't you quit your job while you finish?' she asks. 'If you can afford it and you're doing all the household stuff, why try to work too?' I don't know the answer. 'You're doing too much,' she says.

Later, I'm scrolling Instagram and a post comes up: 'The greatest gift a daughter can give her mother is to alchemize their inherited pain into healing.'[22] My mother taught me how to grow hydrangeas. She also taught me – without meaning to – how to care and who is responsible for care. In part, I am grateful. A generous and resilient way of loving flowed from my grandmother to my mother and down to me. But the reason I hadn't thought about quitting my job was because my mum would never have given up hers. She fought to work and have financial independence at a time when that choice was harder for women. And 1980s feminism taught us both that a career and modern womanhood were one and the same. But I could let Jim support our family financially for the time it took me to finish the book, because writing is work and loving is work, and if I didn't value these forms of labour, who would? I couldn't keep on doing *everything* as a tribute to an idea of womanhood or to my mother. It wouldn't take her struggles away. My mother in the kitchen, an apron tied over her work clothes. My mother waking me, the sky still dark. She kisses me goodbye.

/

Being able to quit my job, even for the year it took me to finish this book, is a sign of my privilege. Most adults supporting a family need to work full-time, and that is especially so for sole-parent families. There are also many low-income families where people must work more than one job, or families where people cannot work due to physical or mental illness. I wish everyone could make the choice I did, but not everyone can.

It makes me think of 'choice feminism' from the early 2000s, which told women their choices were inherently feminist. The logic of that individualist view works only if women make choices from an equal starting point, which we do not. And choosing doesn't necessarily create more freedom, because every woman's choices are 'shaped and constrained by the unequal conditions in which we live'.[23] To say I chose to be Sam's primary carer is true, but that choice was made within the context of a society that still sees childrearing as women's work. The problem with 'choice' is that it places responsibility for success on the individual, whereas feminist issues are structural. Having choice does not remove the need for collective and significant social change.

I spend grim hours online reading about how the intersection of gender and race compounds inequality for women in Aotearoa. It's borne out in the statistics. Wāhine Māori live shorter lives than Pākehā women and rates of 'cardiovascular disease, cancer, respiratory disease, infant mortality, diabetes, and suicide' are significantly higher for Māori than Pākehā.[24] In 2017, mean earnings for wāhine Māori were 15 percent less per hour than for Pākehā women – and Pasifika women earned 21 percent less per hour than Pākehā women.[25] Pākehā women are also more likely to hold higher qualifications than Māori or Pasifika women.[26] In a 2013 survey of sole-parent families, 84.2 percent were 'headed by women, with Māori and Pasifika overrepresented' and over half those families were in poverty.[27] In terms of care work – where this chapter started – research shows that 'wāhine Māori spend more time caring for others in their household and do more voluntary and community work than women from other ethnic groups'.[28] In 2013, wāhine Māori were around twice as likely to live in rented accommodation, be unemployed and have no access to a motor vehicle, when compared with Pākehā women.[29] Alongside all of these statistics, criminal justice reformer Julia Amua Whaipooti (Ngāti Porou) reports that Aotearoa has the highest incarceration rate of Indigenous women in the world.[30] If colonisation and systemic racism were diseases that could be looked up on WebMD, poverty, trauma and failure to thrive would be among their listed symptoms.

But the self-conscious voice in my head tells me that writing about wāhine Māori only as victims of colonisation contributes to the Pākehā story that Māori are without agency. In pre-colonial Māori society, wāhine Māori had rights and protections far beyond those of European women at the time. Wāhine Māori were not regarded as possessions, retained their own names upon marriage, wore similar garments to men and were protected by their whānau and community from spousal violence.[31] Ani Mikaere (Ngāti Raukawa, Ngāti Porou) explains:

> The roles of men and women in traditional Māori society can be understood only in the context of the Māori world view, which acknowledged the natural order of the universe, the interrelationship or whanaungatanga of all living things to one another and to the environment, and the over-arching principle of balance. Both men and women were essential parts in the collective whole, both formed part of the whakapapa that linked Māori people back to the beginning of the world, and women in particular played a key role in linking the past with the present and the future. The very survival of the whole was absolutely dependent upon everyone who made it up, and therefore each and every person within the group had his or her own intrinsic value.[32]

Reading Mikaere, I learn it was the broader connection and interdependence with the collective that allowed wāhine Māori to balance childrearing responsibilities with roles such as leadership.[33] In contrast, English common law at the time stated that women and children were chattels owned by the head of the family – the husband or father.[34] These chattels could be transferred to another man, so when a daughter married, she went from being the property of her father to being the property of her husband. As Mikaere writes of the European woman at this time: 'at best she was incapacitated, only a partial person'.[35] While women are no longer property, remnants of English common law can still be found in Aotearoa law today.[36]

'[T]he only way to foster any shared solidarity is to learn from each other's struggles, and recognise the various privileges and disadvantages that we all enter the movement with,' writes Reni Eddo-Lodge of feminism.[37] It's important to me to own my privilege as a Pākehā woman and the many privileges that come from growing up with food and love and a conventionally acceptable body. Ownership means, at each moment, trying to see how my experiences of womanhood are filtered through the lens of Pākehā culture (both a shelter and a cage). I am trying because '[p]rivilege *saturates*, privilege *structures*' and it is hidden from those who have it.[38] So I offer my experiences for whatever value they have for others – might be some, might be none.

A Pākehā lens also applies to care work, because care is culturally defined. In an article about what unpaid work means to Pasifika communities, Teresa Cowie writes that 'Pasifika do up to 30 hours of unpaid work per week, including about 27,000 hours per week of organised volunteer work for community and church organisations', but that the numbers are probably underreported.[39] This is, Cowie says, because Pasifika peoples do not see their service as unpaid work. As Dr Seini Taufa explains: 'calling service to their family and community "unpaid work" implies a certain amount of burden that they don't feel. It could even be considered offensive.'[40] In this cultural context, women may choose to do more care work rather than less. A wahine Māori friend also pointed out to me that care work doesn't always involve people; the Māori concept of kaitiakitanga and environmental guardianship incorporates ideas of care.

Through the patient teachings of other women, I have learned that being a Pākehā feminist requires me to know in my bones that my beliefs about womanhood will intrinsically support and reproduce systems of Whiteness. As Eddo-Lodge writes:

> Feminism is not about equality, and certainly not about
> slipping silently into a world of work created by and for men.
> Feminism at its best is a movement that works to liberate all

people who have been economically, socially, and culturally
marginalised by an ideological system that has been designed
for them to fail.[41]

Aotearoa writer Max Harris describes a type of White defensiveness called 'detriment-centring' which focuses our country's racism narrative on 'the disadvantages faced by Māori, but without any acknowledgement of the advantages or protection factors which flow from being Pākehā'.[42] Harris writes that 'for those of us who identify as Pākehā, or grew up in Pākehā-dominant spaces, there's a special responsibility to strive to be aware of our own advantages'.[43]

In other words, the suffering and disadvantage caused by the oppression of people of colour cannot be decoupled from the advantage that comes from the wealth, social power and privilege of being Pākehā.[44] Belinda Borell (Ngāti Ranginui, Ngāi Te Rangi, Whakatōhea), Amanda Gregory, Tim McCreanor, Victoria Jensen and Helen Moewaka Barnes (Te Kapotai, Ngāpuhi-nui-tonu) write that 'Privilege refers to systematic and interpersonal advantage that works *in concert* with systemic discrimination and marginalization'.[45] The italics here are my emphasis of their point that privilege and oppression are two ends of the same scale. There are a finite number of business grants, educational scholarships, culturally informed healthcare services, warm homes, well-funded schools, well-paying jobs and positions of political power available to Aotearoa New Zealanders, and most sit on the Pākehā side of the scale.

Looking at it again, the 1980s slogan 'Girls Can Do Anything' does not feel like freedom. Women's right to work outside the home was an incredible step forward for women's liberation, but not if women are expected to do the majority of care work, and not if liberation excludes women who aren't White. For me to continue to believe that women can and must do everything not only harms me, but perpetuates a broken system: it shows my assumption that I am entitled to the resources, space and opportunities required to do everything without owning how much easier it is for me to obtain these things. It doesn't recognise the way that *doing everything* comes from a Pākehā narrative that glamourises individual success, social status, materialism, wealth and economic productivity, and excludes Indigenous and non-White ways of being.

There's more to what novelist Lynn Steger Strong said about the cost of creative work. Here's the quote in full:

> *I would argue that there is nothing more sustaining to long-term creative work than time and space – these things cost money – and the fact that some people have access to it for reasons that are often outside of their control continues to create an ecosystem in which the tenor of the voices that we hear from most often remains similar. It is no wonder, I say often to students, that so much of the canon is about rich white people. Who else, after all, has the time and space to finish a book?*[46]

In the end, I applied to Creative New Zealand and was awarded a writing grant to help finish this book. I wonder whose space I am taking up, and what their voice would say instead. How unlike my own it would be. A year later, I found a new job. And I am still learning how to be a carer without abandoning myself. I don't know the answer to these questions or the others I have about Whiteness and womanhood. I'm letting it be a mess inside me. The only tidy way to be White is through a denial of the privilege and harm of my Whiteness, and I can't do that. I have been thinking about what Makanaka Tuwe writes in her essay 'Projectile Solidarity' on the relationship between social capital, social media and social justice.[47] She argues for an 'embodied experience' of activism and giving ourselves the 'time and space to engage in deep listening' as a way to integrate the different realities of other people. '[L]et's be reminded that transformation happens in and through our *relationships*', she says.[48] While Tuwe is writing from an Indigenous perspective and means all relations – human and non-human – her words make me think about how the relationships we create with ourselves and those we love can be the first sites for change.

When Sam was still just a baby Mum flew up from Ōtautahi for a visit. She sat on the couch drinking tea while I played with Sam on the floor. He had just started smiling and was lying on his back, cooing and waving his pudgy feet in the air. Mum's face saddened for a moment. 'My greatest regret is not being home with you,' she said. I wonder, what am I going to regret? As a woman I have so many options.

Chapter Five
Grotesque bodies

The decision to quit my job meant that when people asked me how work was going I had to admit that I was working on a book. Friends would smile encouragingly, but when I told them the book was about womanhood and middle age their stance shifted. Their brow would crease a little or they'd shuffle their feet. They'd laugh nervously and ask, 'So when does middle age begin again?'

Now I'm in my mid-forties I feel like I've entered middle age. But as I write these words, I realise I've taken for granted that I know what 'middle-aged' means. I don't have a clear idea of when middle age starts or whether it varies from person to person. I don't even know if middle age is something that people experience across different cultures and throughout history. Would my great-grandmother living in that small flat above the bakery in the early twentieth century have thought of herself as middle-aged? Would Mary Evans, my great-grandmother six generations back, who married a boatman called Thomas Rogers in Wolverhampton in 1831 when she was just fourteen, and then had six children in the next twelve years, would she have been thinking about middle age?

After doing some googling, I discover a field of cultural studies called 'age studies' that explores the way we see ageing, including middle age. Reading further, I find cultural anthropologist Richard Shweder, who helpfully defines middle age as that time of life 'roughly' between 'ages 30–70', as culturally European and American, and as an idea based on 'chronological, biological and medical' factors.[1, 2] In other words, whether a woman is middle-aged or not is determined by events in her life such as turning forty or starting menopause. When these events happen, the cultural meanings associated with middle age are laid on top of her personhood, whether they fit or not. As cultural critic Margaret Morganroth Gullette suggests, middle-aged is '[w]henever you begin to believe that Not-Young, the condition that has been lurking about since late adolescence, finally and undeniably manifests itself', such as when you encounter a boy in a sports store who compares you to his mother.[3] People often say to me, 'But you don't look like a mother', or 'You don't look over forty', to which I reply: 'What does a mother look like?' 'What does a woman over forty look like?'

I guess I learned about middle age when I was a teenager. Mum would often get painful migraines and have to lie down in her bedroom. After school I would sneak in to see her, trying to step quietly over the carpet. I knew that noise made the migraines worse. The heavy velvet drapes that she loved so much were drawn tightly across the windows, the room dark and still. Her face was often under the covers, with a small halo of blonde hair fanning out on her pillow. We'd have a short and muffled conversation before I'd sneak out again. She was going through 'the menopause' my father said, crashing around in the kitchen and obviously uncomfortable talking about the topic. Her migraines were hormonal; these things happened to middle-aged women.

In the three decades that followed, no one has *ever* tried to educate me about the experiences of women at midlife. No doctor, nurse, gynaecologist or teacher mentioned menopause, what it's like to age as a woman, or what the middle of my life might be like. At high school, no discussion was had in biology class or sex education of the hormonal and physical changes that happen to women as they age. Most of our time was spent learning about reproduction, the difference between tampons and pads, and being shown how to open and roll on a condom.

While the medical experts in my life were silent, the culture was not. Since my teenage years I've absorbed cruel stories about middle age. Middle-aged women are dumpy and slow. No longer youthful and able to have children, our value to society has diminished. We are ineffective at work, dull in conversation and do not care about sex or an erotic existence, which is lucky for us because we've become invisible to others. I've come into my own middle age with these ideas living inside me. Middle age is to be endured alone in a dark room, under the covers.

/

I'm interested to read that the reason middle age has only recently been studied in depth is because it's a new concept. The term 'middle age' was first used by the upper classes in North America and Britain in the late nineteenth century, and gained wider use at the beginning of the twentieth century. The rise in popularity of the term 'middle age' was buoyed by scientific studies that split human life into stages based on chronological age. The first studies were of 'infancy, childhood and adolescence', which were seen as 'developmental' times in a person's life and therefore positive. As population demographics changed in the twentieth century, the elderly 'were also made subjects of research'. Finally, came studies of 'middle age'.[4]

Before our lives were sectioned using the chronological model that seems so natural today, a person's life stage was measured by their place in their family or their social status. Going further back, life stages in medieval Europe (500–1500 CE) were influenced by Arab and Greek scholars who attributed a 'magical quality' to the number seven. Life-stage transitions happened at multiples of seven: at ages seven, fourteen, twenty-one and so on, and a man was considered in his prime at age forty-nine (seven times seven).[5] Going even further back, during the height of the Roman Empire (27 BCE–286 CE) child labour was common – there is evidence of six-year-old children working as heavy labourers in clothing mills – and girls were married as young as twelve.[6] I doubt middle age as we know it today was much of a concern to those young brides.

The move towards defining a person's life stage by their chronological age was also affected by changes in education in the mid-nineteenth century. The school system in Britain and America slowly moved towards 'age grading', a practice whereby children were grouped and taught by age rather than ability. Age grading was adopted first in cities, where the population meant large numbers of children attended a single school, and then in smaller rural schools.[7] The following description of an American school explains how children were often taught before age grading:

Up to 1855 in Boston, one room in a multiroom building would be for teaching reading, and students would be divided within the room by reading-skill groups, through which they progressed until they had mastered enough material to be sent to another classroom in which writing would be taught.[8]

While age grading started out using 'wide bands', where children close in age were taught in the same grade, the system gradually moved toward grade levels based on birth year.[9] Over time, age grading spread to other organisations such as social clubs and sporting events, as anyone who has entered a marathon and been classed as a 'Master' will know; my local marathon offers five different age grades for participants over forty years. Likewise, Sam recently joined Scouts New Zealand and because he is nine, he was put into Cubs (8–11 years). If he wants to continue on, he'll then move to Scouts (11–14 years), Venturers (14–18 years) and finally Rovers (18–26 years).

I don't think there is anything inherently wrong with using age grading to organise groups of people. Like any system, it has its pros and cons. What I am trying to show is the way age grading has become so widespread and dominant as to be invisible. It's our norm and I didn't think twice about ticking the 'Cubs' box on the Scouts enrolment form. But when a social structure becomes invisible the values and judgements that arise from that structure also are invisible. To paraphrase a speech by David Foster Wallace: '"What water?" said the fish.'[10]

Alongside changes in education, the Second Industrial Revolution (c. 1870–1914) also changed how the West views ageing. The flourishing of capitalism meant that employers began to favour younger men, in both factory settings and office work.[11] With capitalism came a drive for continual technological progress, and the accompanying belief that progress makes the older generation obsolete. Rooted in a Protestant work ethic, a person's worth was linked to their ability to be productive and independent, with dependence being judged negatively.[12] Gullette explains that '[m]en over forty were laid off first from factory work; in the most taxing industries they were wrecks at thirty' and that rapid 'technological changes deskilled older workers', who were then passed over in favour of younger workers.[13] Consequently, in the 1900s men begin to shave on a regular basis. Beards, which up until then had been a symbol of age and wisdom, suddenly went out of fashion as men tried to appear younger to gain and keep employment.[14]

It was also around the beginning of the twentieth century that women's ageing became framed as a problem. Canadian medical anthropologist Margaret Lock writes that while the term 'menopause' came into use in the 1820s – it was first used in print in 1819 by French physician C.P.L. de Gardanne – it was mostly seen as 'a rewarding time' where women, now beyond childbearing age, could use their energy to contribute to the community.[15, 16] The original term for the changes that happen for women at midlife was 'climacteric', meaning 'critical period', which comes from the Greek *klimacter* or 'rung of a ladder'.[17] Women often celebrated this period because in a time without reliable contraception it meant they were no longer at risk of pregnancy. But with the rise of Freudian psychoanalysis at the end of the nineteenth century, menopause came to be seen as a time of depression where the loss of a woman's reproductive ability was equated with a loss of her femininity. It was also now a medically defined syndrome with a set of symptoms after a certain Dr Clouston gave it the name 'Climacteric Insanity' in 1899.[18] Menopause became the central way of telling a woman's story at midlife, and 'virtually obliterated' all other ways of seeing female ageing.[19]

Between 1920 and 1935, women's middle-aged bodies became 'troubling' and 'unwanted'.[20] Even when the psychoanalytic reading of menopause began to lose popularity, other medical, gynaecological and endocrinological narratives took its place to insist that a young body was the 'standard for the bodies of all women'.[21, 22] As Gullette writes, women's bodies at midlife became seen as 'grotesque or pathetic in ways that had not been possible before the cult of youth'.[23]

Novelist Dorthe Nors draws a vivid picture of how middle-aged women are perceived as

women who are no longer young, no longer the sexy one, no longer worth helping out in the subway, no longer worth stopping your car for when she stands there with her grocery bags and her saggy breasts, no longer worth the intellectual conversation, no longer on screen, no longer in the movies, no longer counted, no longer ... somebody – or as I asked an older Swedish *feminist once:* What would you say is the strangest thing about becoming an older woman? *And she answered:* Woman?! I'm no longer a woman, *and then she laughed her heart out ...*[24]

The reason I've outlined the somewhat dry history of middle age is because I want to see myself as somebody, and I refuse to see myself as grotesque or not counting just because I've entered my forties. I hope that at least half of my life is still to come. Understanding how the idea of 'middle age' evolved through arbitrary twists of culture and history helps me place it outside of myself. Looking becomes an act of separation. By seeing where it came from, I can see that it's not me.

/

The other night Sam and I were getting into bed to read a book. It was a warm evening and I was wearing a blouse and some shorts. He pointed to where my bare thigh pressed down against the blanket. 'What's that?' he asked and gestured toward my lumpy, dimpled flesh. I explained cellulite to him, my tone light and informative. I said it was a type of fat. That it was normal and just part of people's bodies. That women have it more than other people, and that people often get more as we age. 'Ah,' he said, suddenly disinterested, and patted one hand on the fantasy book we were about to read.

Normalising my body for Sam is a form of activism, because women's bodies – aged and otherwise – are sites for hatred. Actor Melissa McCarthy (who, over fifty, would be considered middle-aged) was called 'grotesque' by a reporter. Apparently she looked 'sloppy' because she hadn't done her hair for an interview.[25] Her *hair.* (*How dare she?* I imagine the reporter thinking, especially as McCarthy is a woman with the audacity to live happily in a fat body). The comment was meant to humiliate McCarthy, but it did more than that. To call someone grotesque is to say they transgress against what is considered normal and accepted; to be grotesque is to be defined in opposition. In literature, 'the grotesque' has qualities of being both comedic and disgusting. We exaggerate and caricature for entertainment while being repelled at the same time. Frankenstein's lumbering monster; the misshapen Gollum; hunched Quasimodo ringing the bells of Notre Dame. The grotesque is always dehumanising.

Many women who are public figures are dehumanised in this way. A Nike advert showing singer and model Annahstasia's underarm hair was called 'disgusting' by commenters on Instagram.[26] While holding the position of chancellor of Germany, arguably one of the most powerful roles in the world, Angela Merkel was called 'an unfuckable lard ass' by a male politician.[27] In the six-month period running up to the 2017 United Kingdom general election, Diane Abbott, the first Black woman elected to the British parliament, received around 2000 abusive tweets a month, which was almost half of all abusive tweets directed at women MPs during this time.[28] One tweet called her a 'fat disgusting obese chicken-loving n****r'.[29]

To kill or rape a woman is to try to make her grotesque. Anita Sarkeesian, who critiques sexism in video games, was tweeted at: 'I HOPE YOU GET FUCKING RAPED U FUCKING WHORE'. Renowned classics academic Mary Beard, who lectures on the ways men have silenced women across history, received the death threat: 'I'm going to cut off your head and rape it'.[30]

From 2009 to 2015, eighty-one Aotearoa women were killed while leaving their partners.[31] I imagine one is caught at the back door. Another makes it out on to the driveway. Sometimes the women tried to defend themselves by using a weapon readily at hand, most often a kitchen knife. Before being silenced, the women often inflicted a wound on their attacker. Reading this information in the Family

Violence Death Review Committee's *Fifth Report Data* I want to yell, 'Fuck him up!' but this is no serial killer show on TV. Why do I watch those anyway? Why do I need to see women twisted, smeared and dirty and discovered in a forest?

In over half of the deaths the men performed 'overkill'. I say 'men' because nearly all of the offenders were men.[32] 'Overkill' is the technical term for excessive violence where a killer does not seek only to kill their victim, but also aims to desecrate and obliterate.

Maybe I watch those serial killer shows as a type of preparation. They allow me, while tucked safely under a blanket in my lounge, to think about how I'd respond in a similar situation. When Sam was six months old a man stumbled out of the bush reserve that spreads green and dense below our house. I could hear him huffing and talking to himself as he moved up around the side of the house. His head blurred across the window of my bedroom. He was moments from our front door when I scrambled to lock it. He tried the handle. It went up and down. I crouched down on the floor so he couldn't see me. I yelled that my husband was home, my voice wobbling. I yelled that I was calling the police. Maybe he was homeless. He seemed drunk and confused and his clothes and face were dirty. But my baby son was asleep in his room, and if this man had broken into the house I would have been prepared to kill him. I had already taken a knife from the kitchen drawer.

A few months ago, I was walking down a set of narrow pedestrian steps near the Botanic Gardens. Although the morning was clear, it had rained the night before and the steps were still wet. A man came into view and started walking up towards me, and even from a distance I could see his broad shoulders, large arms and thick neck. Where we'd meet on the steps was a tight corridor of trees and fences. Jasmine grew wild and the heady scent hung in the air. As the man passed me his foot slipped on a step and his body fell toward me. I cried out – a strangled sound – and flinched back. He righted himself. He didn't look at me and kept on walking. I thought about this man for days afterward and how terrified I was of him. How from the moment he entered the steps I felt worried. I thought about how my guttural cry must have made him feel. He was just a man walking home, but I don't know who to be afraid of any more.

Journalist Kate Maltby describes how Elizabeth I – arguably the most powerful woman in British history – has been repeatedly depicted on screen as 'the epitome of the female grotesque'.[33] Her balding head, her white-caked face, her aged and childless body. To connect society's disgust of women's aged bodies with the way women are murdered may seem a leap, but they both exist on a continuum of control. Whether she is alive or dead, to label a woman grotesque is to try and deny her humanity and power.

/

While researching the origins of middle age, I found examples of how middle age is seen in non-Western cultures. I was interested to learn that in 'Japan, India, Samoa, Kenya and among African-Americans in the United States' middle age did not or does not exist.[34] Instead, the way a woman transitions through adulthood can be understood through life stages based on the social roles she holds in a 'kinship group', extended family or community; a woman's social standing and associated responsibilities determine life stage, rather than her chronological age.[35] As Shweder states – pointing towards the way Western culture views itself as standard – many cultures recognise 'mature adulthood … without ritual celebration of a fortieth birthday party'.[36]

In her essay 'Deconstructing the Change' Margaret Lock explores how Japanese women have traditionally transitioned through life stages based on 'a social process involving community rituals', with the 'locus' of these rituals more recently shifting to the family. For these women, the transition to adulthood happens with marriage and then ends at age sixty when she ritually passes into old age.[37] While Western culture focuses on the linear journey of '*individuals* as they age', Lock writes that Japanese culture focuses on the 'changing *social relationships*' of women.[38] Traditionally, Japanese women construct their identity in terms of social structure – families and communities – and see themselves as one part of the cycle of generations. As Lock explains, in Japan middle age was 'understood as a relatively undifferentiated part of the life cycle'.[39]

To look specifically at menopause, in traditional Sino-Japanese medicine the end of menstruation was called *tenki* and was seen as the seventh stage in a woman's life, but there was no specific term for the broad experience of menopause.[40] By the end of the nineteenth century, the term *kōnenki* was used for the life stage during which menopause occurs.[41] Lock argues that *kōnenki* conveys the biological changes that happen in a woman's endocrine system, but also broader 'disturbances' to the nervous system that occur with ageing.[42] Menopause and the decline of reproduction is part of *kōnenki*, but not its defining factor. While Japanese women have hot flashes and night sweats – symptoms which epitomise menopause and middle age in Western cultures – they are reported at lower rates; women in Japan tend to report 'stiffness, headaches, [and] dizziness' instead.[43] Lock explains that '*kōnenki* and menopause are not the same concept', and implies that because menopause is not viewed as a medical condition to be separated from the other biological realities of ageing, Japanese women experience it differently.

One aspect that may contribute to the way Japanese women experience ageing is the tradition that mature women cultivate an art form. Women are encouraged to develop themselves through practices like ikebana or calligraphy, which don't rely on a young or mobile body. The tradition is based in Zen Buddhism and the Confucian idea that all people can work towards 'human perfectibility over time', irrespective of age.[44] It is also supported by the traditional Japanese view that a person gains 'wisdom, authority, and a hard-won freedom to be flexible and creative' as they age.[45] Whereas women in the West often feel invisible as they age, Japanese women are encouraged to flourish, change and become playful – they are able to let go of the 'feminine reserve' that their earlier life required.[46] In Japan, ageing is seen not as a decline but a natural process that relates to social maturation.

I also learned that, similar to Japanese culture, Sāmoan culture determines a person's life stage by their social standing and roles. There were five life stages in traditional Sāmoan society: '*pepe* (baby/infant), *tama'ititi* (child), *tagata talavou* (youth), *tagata matua* (adult), and *toea'ina* or *lo'omatua* (old man or woman)'.[47] Bradd Shore writes that chronological age was less important to adult Sāmoans than other life markers such as social status, political status and being seen as having mature judgement. Mature adulthood was viewed as a 'transition between two kinds of status: that associated with physical work and movement and that associated with passive authority'.[48] Instead of the Western story of decline, mid-adulthood was seen as the stage of life where social and political power came together. While 'middle-aged' Sāmoans also dealt with the changes that came with physical ageing and a 'growing awareness of their own mortality', it was not seen as a time of crisis.[49] A woman moved from adulthood into old age not when she passed a certain chronological age, but when she became dependent on others for care, whether that be at fifty or eighty-five.

As part of the 2014 research study 'Pacific Perspectives on Ageing in New Zealand', Taimalie Kiwi Tamasese, Tafaoimalo Loudeen Parsons and Charles Waldegrave asked Sāmoan elders about their perceptions of ageing. The researchers used fa'afaletui, a Sāmoan concept which describes a method of gathering and validating important knowledge.[50] In their fa'afaletui, the Sāmoan elders shared that '[e]ldership is perceived ... based on maturity of judgement or *Moe o le Tofa*, rather than being about age or physical ageing', and that eldership was not defined by age but instead could be understood as 'two specific groupings – those who are not so active and being cared for by their families or *Matua tausi* and those who are active and largely independent elder women *Olomatua* and men *Toeaina*'. The women's fa'afaletui expressed that ideas of 'the aged and the elderly' in New Zealand are 'social constructs' that attribute certain constraints and limits to ageing and that, in their view, prevent them from 'living life fully ... and did not take into account their own realties'.[51]

I am coming to these accounts about what it is like to be a middle-aged or older woman living in Japan or Sāmoa as an outsider who cannot understand the specificity of those experiences. Some of the accounts are generalisations based on research undertaken during a particular time (and in the cases of Shore and Lock, by academics from outside of these cultures). Globalisation has seen Western cultural values seep into other cultures, including the concept of 'middle age'.[52] For instance, modern Japanese culture has moved towards Western individualism, which has seen a rise in *kōnenki* being medicalised. Since the 1970s, the ageing population in Japan has also 'prompted a range of narratives' that are often negative and disproportionally affect women.[53] Just as we do gender norms, we learn 'age categories', and what each category represents for us comes from 'a complex mix of generational meanings, broader cultural meanings, and historically situated personal experiences'.[54] While the concept of 'middle age' did not exist in rural Sāmoa in the 1970s, it seems much more likely that it does now.

I am also not trying to suggest that one cultural experience of womanhood is better than another – while Japanese women may see ageing more positively than their sisters in the West, it should be noted that this is in the context of a culture that, at least historically, tends to be male-dominated and with paternalistic tendencies. Such a culture limits women's choices, and the expectation that women will focus on family seems stronger for Japanese women than Western women. Sāmoan women also face their own issues: a 2018 commission of inquiry found that '[s]ix out of ten women [living in Sāmoa] experience intimate partner violence and one in five is raped', and that village councils were complicit in maintaining silence around the issue.[55]

What I am trying to make visible is that the stories I have absorbed about womanhood and middle age are just that: cultural stories. And there are stories of power for Western women in midlife that I'm not acknowledging – the archetypes of crone, hag and wise woman. The Wicked Witch of the East in *The Wizard of Oz*; terrifying Baba Yaga; Bellatrix Lestrange – even if evil or grotesque, this crone figure is the one who 'can work magic'.[56] I've been joking to friends that in the next phase of my life I want to be a 'garden witch', and it only occurred to me recently that I'm drawing on these tropes of female power. The power is limited, though. To have this power is to exist on the margins, to be solitary, angry and haggish. I keep on thinking about what my friend Nicola said of being fifty-six: 'I feel like I'm coming up on a pretty powerful part of my life.' I hope so. There is a freedom that comes with no longer being seen as an object. I can turn towards a deeper connection with myself and others, and my presence and authority can come from experience and compassion.[57]

Ageing is not only a social process; there are biological realities that women face as we age. All women start to stiffen and creak. Our skin becomes papery and thin, and sits a little looser on our bodies. Our organs struggle to be as effective as when they were brand new. Our bones become brittle, spines shorter and our muscle mass dwindles. Our hair follicles run out of pigment cells and grow locks a shimmery grey. Cisgender women go through menopause, with its changes to hormones, menstruation and body fat. The number of nerve cells in our brain decreases. The lenses in our eyes harden and yellow, and our hearing worsens after decades of noise. *What did you say?* we ask. *Can you pass me my glasses?* Since turning forty, I get injured more easily, my running times are slower and I've developed arthritis in my spine. Last week I pulled a muscle in my shoulder while making the bed. All of these things are happening to me. But the perception that these changes make me less valuable as a woman creates a secondary and more painful experience than the ageing itself.

I have found that my experience of midlife depends on how compassionately I can welcome these changes. How completely I can unclench my need for control. I have little advice on how to do this. Some days I greet my ageing face like a friend. I smile at her in the bathroom mirror. *Who are you?* I ask, because I am genuinely curious about who she will become. On other days, I forget. Sam and I wait in line at the local dairy. It's a blustery, hot afternoon and we're buying some popsicles on the way home from the beach. We've spent a few hours walking a friend's dog along the sand, Sam running down to the surf, the dog chasing after him. Now we're tired and ready for home. In the dairy he takes a long time to choose a popsicle, sliding his body over the cooler as he looks at the colourful rows; opening and closing the cooler door. Finally he decides on lemon and lime. As I hold the cold blocks in my hand waiting to pay, I notice he's looking at me. 'What's up?' I ask. He smiles. 'Your tummy is bigger,' he says. My body stiffens. I feel a flush of humiliation and shame across my cheeks – everyone waiting heard what he said but has looked away, pretending they didn't. 'Ah ha,' I say. I put my arm around him, but he knows I'm upset.

'What's wrong, Mama?' he asks when we get in the car. 'Nothing,' I say. As we drive the few minutes home I don't look at him. I feel tears prickling my eyes and in my chest an edge of grief. I wish I didn't feel this way, react this way. I don't want to give him confusing messages about what it's okay to be or say, and I know he'll believe the one I tell with my body. And my body feels angry and ashamed. After we park I calmly turn around. He's in the back seat, his eyes unsure as he takes tiny bites of his popsicle. I reach one arm back so I can take his hand. I try to explain that I was upset by his comment, but that there's nothing wrong with our bodies changing. That it's normal and okay. That all bodies are okay. 'I know that,' he says, confused that I am telling him something I've said before. I try to explain that sometimes we don't feel okay about things that are okay. I say it again, mostly for myself. We don't always feel okay about things that are okay.

/

While researching middle age, the most interesting study I found had the misleadingly dull title 'Perceptions of Aging across 26 Cultures and their Culture-Level Associates'. The research explores the way 'ideas, values, and customs related to aging' translate into beliefs and expectations about ageing.[58] These 'culture-level' ideas, which are often seen by those who hold them as universal experiences, influence how a culture tells stories about ageing, which in turn affects how individuals living in that culture experience ageing. Bear with me.

The study, which surveyed college students from twenty-six cultures across six continents, asked respondents how their culture viewed different aspects of ageing.[59] The questions focused primarily on two types of ageing: the biological changes that happen as we age, and changes that happen to our emotional and family life and life satisfaction.[60] Nearly all respondents reported that ageing was viewed negatively by their culture, with 'widespread cross-cultural consensus' that the categories of 'physical attractiveness' and 'ability to do everyday tasks' decreased with age.[61] There was also consensus that categories such as 'wisdom' and 'respect' were seen to increase with age.[62]

The study found that most of the differences in the ways cultures perceive ageing were explained by sociodemographic factors. For example, high economic development and industrialisation of a culture directly corresponded to negative views of ageing. Negative views were especially likely if the country also had high levels of education enrolment and a large population of people aged over sixty-five. The reasons for these results aren't entirely clear, but one possibility is that urbanisation and the ability to relocate globally have undermined traditional knowledge-passing between generations. A few hundred years ago most people grew up, married and lived their adult lives close to where they were born. As young people depend less upon the older members of their family, their social bonds weaken.[63] Unsurprisingly, young people who spent time with older members of their community had a more positive view of ageing.[64]

The one result in perceptions of ageing that could not be explained by sociodemographic factors was that of 'National Character Stereotype'. Respondents were asked to report on the 'stereotypical perceptions of the personality traits of a "typical" member of their culture'.[65] Those who described typical members of their culture 'as open, agreeable, and low in Neuroticism' also reported that their culture viewed ageing more positively, *independent* of sociodemographic factors.[66] This was closely connected to another result: people who viewed their culture as having high levels of 'Uncertainty Avoidance' (or an inability to tolerate doubt and ambiguity) reported negative views of ageing.[67]

I won't describe a 'typical member' of Aotearoa culture. I don't believe there is such a thing, and it would be a disservice to the social and cultural diversity that exists here. What seems more important than a cultural stereotype is the idea the research reveals: it's not only how we see our own ageing that matters, but how we think people around us will judge it. The reason I found Sam's comments in the dairy confronting was because I feared the people standing in line would judge me negatively. Imagine how different my experience would have been if I'd expected understanding and acceptance. It reminds me that most of my fears arise from the fear of being seen and, after being seen, of being rejected. It reminds me that – no matter how someone else reacts – only I can reject myself. Only I can allow them to make me grotesque.

It's exhausting to be in constant dialogue with society's idea of who women should be. And I often worry that my small disruptive acts of self-acceptance won't change me or the larger world. But as Eleanor Gordon-Smith says, 'The point with these sorts of efforts isn't to measure them by what success they're likely to have. The point is to practise a way of engaging with the world that takes us out of ourselves and into something bigger.'[68] And when my son and I read together in my bed, his pale skinny legs hooked around mine, our bodies fallen in place against each other, his hand often seeks out a soft part of me, an arm or a thigh, because for him softness means comfort. And as he listens to my voice, I feel like maybe that's enough.

Chapter Six
The crossing

My friend Leslie and I walk the Tongariro Crossing. The nineteen-kilometre track traces a saddle between the volcanic peaks of Ngāuruhoe and Tongariro in central Te Ika-a-Māui, circles the broad-domed summit of Tongariro and then zigzags down its northern slope. Ngāuruhoe and Tongariro rest beside Mt Ruapehu, the three mountains forming the southern limit of the Pacific Ring of Fire – a circlet of volcanoes that extends through the Solomon Islands, the Philippines, Japan, the eastern sea border of Russia and along the west coast of the Americas.

The Tongariro Crossing is one of the most popular walks in Aotearoa, but I'm still nervous. Every year people die on the mountain. Usually they become lost after venturing off the track, especially when the weather turns and cloud rolls across the plateau. The name Tongariro means 'taken by the cold southerly wind', and even on the sunniest day the chill wind can cut through clothing and down to skin.

We leave early on Waitangi Day and drive up the Kāpiti Coast. The road is nearly empty and the beach settlements that hug the shore are still asleep in the silvery morning. After a few hours we reach the cheerful towns of Foxton and Bulls, and turn inland. Lush green farmland glides past the window. We're taking advantage of the public holiday to spend a long weekend away. Leslie drives us in her station wagon, our tramping packs wedged together in the boot. In the back are two empty child booster seats.

I met Leslie at a party before either of us had children. At the time she taught high-school English, and our conversation was easy and immediate. She's a smart, sweet-faced blonde American who met an Aotearoa man in Mexico and eventually moved to Te Whanganui-a-Tara. Years after the party, she and that man bought a two-storey house down the road from me. We each had our first child around the same time, and we both joined the same local mothers' group. We'd sit and talk in each other's lounges, our babies gurgling. Leslie and I occasionally walked the hills of our neighbourhood. We talked about politics (her relatives voted for Trump and mine for Brexit), about mental health and poetry and the status a woman loses when she stays home with her children. Eventually, when our children were old enough to leave for a few days, we started to walk in the mountains.

Mid-afternoon we arrive in Ohakune and pull up to the cabin where we'll spend two nights. The shingled wood structure has silvered with age. Inside we find mismatched furniture, wooden beams and a tiny pot-bellied stove. Hundreds of visitors have carved their names into the kitchen table, right down to the chipboard. 'Let's take a look around,' I say. We crunch back down the gravel drive and out to the middle of the road. Ohakune is a small rural town so there's little traffic. 'Fingers crossed for good weather tomorrow,' Leslie says. I pull my jacket tight around my shoulders. My eyes follow the long straight road into the distance until it merges with layers of bush and then the massive grey form of Ruapehu. Behind, beyond seeing, lies Tongariro.

/

The next morning we rise in the dark. It's cold this close to the mountains so I turn on the cabin's only heater. It whirrs comfortingly. We take turns to shower, and I close my eyes as the hot water blankets my body. We eat at the kitchen table. Leslie works her way through a bowl of porridge and two boiled eggs. 'Double breakfast,' she says. She's wearing a peach t-shirt and walking shorts. She's already laced on her tramping boots. I make two pots of coffee, pour one into a thermos for later and sit with her while I eat my eggs. I worry them around the plate.

After we've eaten, we check and recheck our packs in a pre-walk ritual. I take bundled-up clothes out just to put them back in again. Three litres of water and enough food to last twenty-four hours. A silver emergency blanket. A back-up cellphone battery. An emergency kit. A head torch. We have a conversation about whether or not Leslie should take two pairs of shoes. I like being here in this quiet cabin with another woman, the sky dark, no one asking anything of me.

We drive through the pale morning out of Ohakune to Tohunga Junction, and then past Horopito and National Park. The long stretches of road are edged intermittently by pine forests and fields ready for harvest, some already taken back to bare earth. We turn onto Highway 47, which snakes along the green base of Ngāuruhoe and Tongariro. The land flashes by. The sunrise flares white and orange behind the mountains, turning the slopes dusky and mysterious. Our car is a tiny creature inching through the landscape.

Leslie navigates our route on Google Maps as I drive. I have a tight feeling in my stomach. Is it anxiety? I know I am worried that we won't get to the parking lot on time and we'll miss our shuttle. 'I think I've taken a wrong turn,' I say and pull onto the gravel shoulder of the road. We both lean over Leslie's phone and try to make the shapes line up with the landscape outside the window. 'You're going the right way,' Leslie says and gives me a smile as if to say, *You're okay*. I pull back out on the road.

I wonder if I'm anxious because I'm away from Sam. While he no longer needs the constant, consuming care a young child does, I habitually look for him. In the cabin that morning I thought I saw his back disappear through a doorway. While eating breakfast I started to my feet when I heard a child cry out from a nearby house, a moment before realising that the child wasn't mine. It's not lost on me that placing all my attention and care on my son is a way to bypass my own feelings – something that women are taught to do. It's socially accepted and praised to put aside what I need and want in favour of my child. *You're such a good mother*, other women say to me. I hope so, but also during Sam's early years forgetting myself was sometimes the only way I could get through the day until, with a wash of relief, I heard Jim walking down our steps.

And it's not that I have become a *mother* in place of the woman who liked to read in bed all day on a Saturday, or see a movie by herself in the afternoon, or have her husband lie behind her during sex so when she pulled him into her it felt both erotic and comforting. It is just more difficult to find time for the selfish and indulging parts of myself. As Maggie Nelson writes of motherhood, 'difficulty in shifting gears, or a struggle to find the time, is not the same thing as an ontological either/or'.[1]

But when the space and time to be with myself do open up – such as in a cabin in a small mountain town – I am restless, panicky. The woman I was before having Sam has been changed by the experience. *Who will I find now? What if I don't like her? What if being her means Sam loves me less?* Just as learning to care for Sam was a transition that required bravery, so is learning not to care so fully and how to turn my attention back towards myself.

Halfway through our drive, we stop the car for a herd of sheep. Two men on quad bikes are moving the animals down the road. The men stand upright, gloved hands gripping the handlebars as they call out to each other. One of the men works the edge of the herd so it flows in a single direction, instinct pulling the animals forward. The other pushes from behind. We wind down our windows as the sheep stream past the car. Their hooves clatter on the asphalt and the sun shines white off their woolly backs. 'Maybe we did bring too much gear,' Leslie says as we watch the sheep move past. She's looking out the window and fidgeting with her hands. I suddenly realise that she's anxious, too. These three days will be the longest stretch of time she's been away from her children, both of whom are younger than Sam. She must also be feeling that strange unsettling combination of exhilaration and anxiety. I feel a rush of tenderness for my friend. 'We're good,' I say, 'we're well-prepared women,' and then the sheep clear and the mountain waits before us and we go.

/

Even though I loved tramping as a child, from my late teens until my forties I didn't like being in the wilderness. My friends would pull over to do a bush walk if we were driving home from a weekend away. As they tramped to a waterfall or a giant kauri, I'd roll down a window and wait it out in the car. This was before each of us had a smartphone in our pocket, so I couldn't even distract myself. I'd simply wait, restless in my seat, feeling disconnected and sad until they returned. There was something about the uncontained nature of the bush that made me uncomfortable, maybe because I was trying to contain so much of myself during those years.

In my forties, it suddenly changed. Seemingly overnight, I developed a hunger to be in the bush and mountains. I began to google walking tracks close to Te Whanganui-a-Tara and to read through the descriptions on the DOC website. I discarded all tracks that were 'suitable for families'. The walk couldn't be too short or flat – I needed it to be challenging. I wanted to test myself, which meant there must be some survival aspect such as a hut where I'd spend the night and a requirement to carry food and other supplies. I wanted to feel a little remote, a little unsafe, a little wild.

It wasn't until I read the essay '"Midway on our life's journey …".: On psychological transformation at midlife' by Murray Stein that I began to understand my urge to be wild. Stein writes that midlife often begins 'a profoundly transformational period' during which we outgrow our first adult identity so a second, more authentic identity can emerge.[2] Such a transformation often requires a withdrawal from society, which for me meant being in the wilderness. Stein argues that when we first enter adulthood our overwhelming need is to be accepted, in part because after leaving our family of origin we are now in charge of feeding ourselves, paying rent and making sure we stay alive. This is always easier with the support of others. As fledgling adults, our need to belong is so acute that we often, unconsciously, create our identity based on the people around us to make sure we fit in.

Reading Stein, I was reminded of being fresh out of home and starting a degree at Canterbury University. During orientation week, I fell in with a group of goth undergrads who, under the guise of a campus club, spent their time playing cards and listening to 80s music. They seemed edgy and sophisticated to me. They had a certain laissez-faire air, skipping lectures and holding two-day parties at the weekend. They exuded a cool, fuck-the-system confidence, which I can now recognise as middle-class privilege. But back then they seemed free of the heavy self-doubt I carried. I would watch them walk around the university in a group, their bodies willowy and fluid. They seemed made of lust and recklessness. I wanted nothing more than to be like them, which was a much better option than being myself. I dyed my hair black in my flat's bathroom sink. I bought CDs of the Sisters of Mercy and Nine Inch Nails. When I was around them, I talked reverentially about the fashion in *The Matrix*, which back then epitomised goth cool. A photo taken of me two years later shows a young woman in a flowing black dress and combat boots. She has one hand around the neck of a wine bottle. Her other hand is touching the face of a boy wearing black lace gloves. They're at a party, which is what they do. They haven't been to lectures in months. While mimicking others may deliver social acceptance, it is nearly always at the cost of ourselves.

One of the books I brought with me to read in Ohakune was *Beyond the Gender Binary* by Alok Vaid-Menon. They grew up in College Station, a small town in Texas, as part of a close-knit Indian community who would often come together for potluck dinners. When Vaid-Menon was a child, they would put on a show when the families gathered together. 'I used to take my mom's and sister's clothes and promenade around the living room dancing and singing to the latest Bollywood hits,' they write.[3] But when Vaid-Menon performed a similar routine at a first-grade talent show, they were told, 'Boys don't do that.' 'The whole auditorium laughed at me,' they write. 'I learned about gender through shame.'[4]

The constant bullying Vaid-Menon experienced because of their gender expression meant they tried to fit other people's expectations of them. They 'threw out all the pinks and florals' from their closet and instead wore dark colours and cargo shorts.[5] They tried to deepen their voice to sound more like the boys at school. They continued hiding themselves well into young adulthood, and eventually left College Station at age eighteen. 'You edit yourself, and at some point it becomes so normal that you can't even tell that you're doing it,' they write.[6]

While Vaid-Menon's need to edit themselves was due to gender policing and bigotry – and a fear of how bigotry often escalates into violence against trans people – I can't help but find kinship with their experience. I also was a young adult convinced by shame that I was doing my gender wrong. Looking back, I am not surprised; I grew up with a parent who, for decades, lived with gender shame and dysphoria. I eagerly tried to embody the paradox of 90s womanhood: to be smart yet unthreatening; sexy yet chaste; tough yet vulnerable. Or as a friend quipped recently, 'That easy-going chill girlfriend that we all strived to be.' Black hair or otherwise, my costumes of womanhood have always had the same goal: to make me good enough.

And now, in my forties, how do I tell the difference between what is mine and what I've borrowed? Because if my experience of early adulthood was one of editing myself to fit in, then this stage of my life – and the transformation that Stein suggests – feels like a process of returning. For the twentieth anniversary of *The Matrix*, in 2019, I watched the film again with a friend. We settled on the couch, our snacks on the coffee table. As the orchestral music of the opening scene filled the lounge, I felt electric. Maybe it was nostalgia for a young woman who, even while hiding, had moments of powerful freedom? She's still part of me. Maybe it's because I haven't fully let go of the hope that being perfect will save me? What I did know was that I couldn't wait to see Trinity, her hair slicked back. To see her pose on a rooftop, sleek and unmovable in shiny black latex. To see her casually backflip around a spray of bullets. To see her kiss Neo in a shower of sparks.

/

When we reach the track's end I park on the edge of the highway. A line of cars stretches down the road. People are pulling their packs out of car boots, putting on jackets and adjusting straps. We've parked at the end of the track so that when we finish the walk all we'll have to do is slide our tired and dusty bodies back into the car and drive home. From a grassy verge we catch the mountain shuttle that takes us to the start of the crossing.

The shuttle drops us at the top of Mangatepopo Valley. Groups of walkers queue for the toilet block or stand near the carved waharoa that marks the start of the track. We head for a small information shelter and do one last check of our packs. Excited, we lean together and I take a selfie. My lips are parted as though I am laughing; Leslie's blonde hair is pulled back, her eyes crinkled at the edges.

I have another photo taken on the same spot many years before. My body leans into a man and we both have our hoods pulled tight around our faces. The background of the photo is hazy with rain. The first time I tried to walk the crossing a cyclone barrelled across Te Ika-a-Māui. The man who misses my pussy and I made it an hour along the track before, wet to our skin, we turned back.

I also tried to walk the crossing again after that relationship ended. Even though I knew it was too far into autumn for the track to be safe, a part of me needed to try. If I could walk the crossing by myself I'd be able to do everything else without him. But when I arrived in Ohakune snow lay thick on the ground. The kind woman at the information centre told me there were avalanche warnings for the area. That day I didn't even make it to the mountain.

To burn off my sadness I ran around the streets of Rangataua, a small settlement near Ohakune where I'd rented a house. Each time I reached the house – pale blue weatherboards, an overgrown rangy camellia – I'd start another loop of the township. Again past the old microwave turned into a letterbox. Again past the shuttered ski shop with a hand-painted Harrods sign. Again past the single horse grazing in a paddock. I ran all morning.

'Ready?' Leslie asks. She's standing under the waharoa waiting for me.

Over the first few kilometres we stop often. I can't get the heel of my tramping sock right and I keep pausing to shift it around in my shoe. The left strap of Leslie's pack is hurting her shoulder. We're not feeling confident, settled. During one stop we step off the track and let two older women pass. They must be in their sixties and they're moving fast. They power by us, sweatbands smoothing back their grey hair, shin protectors strapped to their legs. They confidently swing their walking poles. 'Let's follow them,' Leslie says, and we fall in behind as they make their way up the valley.

The wide rocky track cuts up the lower slopes. The tussock and scrubby bush that edge the track spread out to create a green and golden patchwork across the landscape. It ripples in the wind. 'There!' I say, and point to where Ruapehu soars above a ridgeline, hints of snow on the summit. The sky is a clear blue, the sun hot above us.

We begin to find our rhythm. As the track narrows, I walk in front and Leslie steps in behind. Our boots crunch in unison, a two-woman percussion section making its way up the valley. Slowly the landscape changes and becomes steeper. We push our way up steps built into a rock face. We reach a series of boardwalks that lift us above the delicate alpine moss and daisies which grow along the channels of water. After an hour of walking we pass Soda Springs, where the water flows vertically off the mountain and down to feed beds of buttercups and foxgloves. The air tastes fresh and clean. My body feels warm and loose.

Apart from our footfalls and the buzz of insects, the mountain is quiet. We stop talking and simply move together. It will be a long day and we both prepare for the effort. I can feel Leslie stepping behind me, an invisible line holding us together, two women moving into the mountain.

/

Once a week I visit Daphne, an elderly woman who lives in my neighbourhood. She's in her eighties and because she's had ministrokes she doesn't leave her house any more. It's the house where she and her husband brought up their children, but now as a widow she lives there alone. There's a large vegetable patch in the back yard and a camellia tree that flowers crimson in autumn. There are pots full of pansies on the front porch. Being stuck at home makes for a lonely existence, which is why I visit. Once a day a carer comes to help her with the cooking and washing, and her son pops around in the evening, but most of the time she sits in the sitting room and listens to the radio.

During my visits we play cards. Usually we play gin rummy, a card game where you build up sets or runs with the goal being to get the most points. Even though she sometimes forgets the rules, she usually wins. When she was a young woman, Daphne worked as an accountant and was a competitive hockey player. She also helped manage her husband's business. One day, after losing another game, I say, 'You must have been formidable when you were younger.' Daphne, not one for sentimentality, looks out the window. 'I was,' she says.

The first time I visited Daphne, I noticed the display cabinets in her hallway. While most of the house had been emptied of furniture in slow preparation for her eventual move to a rest home, these two large cabinets were bursting with knick-knacks. There was a shelf of polished tropical shells. Another was packed with porcelain figurines of young women in meadows, grazing deer and other bucolic scenes. Shelves further down held souvenir spoons, thimbles and ticket stubs. I was there for Daphne so I didn't stop long to look at the shelves, but I felt curious at their busy fullness in the empty house.

Quite a few visits after that first one, I need to use her bathroom. I pad my way up the carpeted stairs and find the door. It's cool inside, and I move the safety frame away from the toilet and sit down. It's then that I notice a huge display shelf on the opposite wall. Each shelf is lined with handmade objects. A bowl with 'World's Best Grandma' stamped near its rim sits beside a painted papier-mâché cat face, which sits beside a wonky urn, a child's thumb print still visible in the clay. The display takes up at least half the wall. Everything is covered with dust. Sitting on the toilet, I think that these must be gifts from her children and grandchildren over the years. And then I get it. For Daphne, her memories live in these objects.

I am thinking about Daphne because I'm trying to understand the way ageing and experience make us more psychologically complex, and I find the metaphor of a home and what it contains a useful way to think about the self. My gothy young self in her early twenties could hitch a trailer to her Toyota Corolla hatchback, load it up with everything she owned, and within a few hours she'd have moved flats. Once she did this four times in a year. All she needed was a single room. She would neatly set up her bed and a small shelf of literature and art books. She'd screw together her wooden bedside table that was shaped like a crescent moon and hang her Christine Webster print on the wall.

Now, my middle-aged self lives in a three-bedroom house with a husband, son and two cats. This self has accumulated various collections. There are shelves of books and ceramics. There's the precious box of Sam's baby clothes. There is a small collection of works on paper – the landscape in the bedroom that our friends bought us when we got married; the typography poster in the hallway from when we bought the house; an illustration from an old book that we found in an odds-and-ends store. There are also house plants, and crafting materials, and toys, and old papers, and a basement full of useful things: woodworking tools, a lawnmower and weed whacker, paint tins and some storage boxes that have sat unopened since our move twelve years ago. None of it is worth very much, but each object in my house reminds me of a time or moment: a past self that led to this self.

More important than quantity in this metaphorical home – because those who live minimalist or nomadic lives can be complex people too – is the presence of contradiction, dissonance and not-sureness. And what is maturity if not that? My bookshelf holds the pulpy science-fiction novels I read as a teenager as well as those art books. My closet carries florals and prints and gold shoes as well as some black dresses. And while we've renovated bits of the house (I painted our ceilings while three months pregnant), the bathroom sink is cracked and the tap handle broke off years ago. A friend of mine commented recently that she was surprised, knowing me as she does, that I'd never had it fixed. But that's because my home doesn't add up to a neat picture of a person, because I am no longer neat.

Murray Stein argues that the midlife transformation happens *because* our growing complexity can no longer be contained within that simple and often borrowed young adult self. While our first identity buoys us through life for a while, it stops serving us, Stein writes, 'when the self calls for more breadth and depth in the personality and in life experience' than our identity can hold.[7] Stein continues:

> For this reason, and in order to become whole and stable
> enough to live successfully into old age … a person must create
> another type of identity. Midlife is precisely the time when
> the personality features required for this come to the fore and
> indeed demand attention.[8]

To put this another way, we must grow to contain the insights and self-understanding that time and experience bring. The result is a midlife transformation that happens, according to Stein, in three phases, and that – to loosely continue the house metaphor – we enter 'through the doorway of loss', whether that be the death of a parent, a divorce, or the sudden crushing understanding that comes when a young man in a sports store likens you to his mum.[9]

During the first phase we withdraw from our communities in order to grieve not only the particular loss – the parent, the marriage, our youth – but a new understanding that arises: things are impermanent and we ourselves are mortal. Stein writes that the sense of invincibility we carried from childhood into young adulthood falls away and we realise our time is limited. We also realise there is no going back. I often find myself thinking about how I let myself down or abandoned myself in order to belong. The work of the first phase and its withdrawal is to feel that grief – for the losses we have suffered, for our youth and naive innocence, but also for the years during which we denied parts of ourselves.

Grieving gives way to the second phase of our transformation – a liminal time where we feel we have no fixed identity. Our younger self, often confident and sure, cannot encompass what we've learned about ourselves, our weirdness and contradictions, and the new mortality we feel. One theorist defines liminality as the 'moments or periods of transition during which the normal limits to thought, self-understanding and behaviour are relaxed, opening the way to novelty and imagination, construction and destruction';[10] another as the points 'neither here nor there; they are betwixt and between'.[11] During this time our sense of self becomes free-floating and inconsistent.

The second phase, Stein writes, also often comes with a burst of energy which, when used well, allows us to experiment with new activities, work, relationships and routines. We can use that energy to create a life that our expanded self can fully inhabit. If the energy is used in an unskilled way it can result in impulsive decisions and the colloquial 'midlife crisis'. When crisis happens it is because we do not stay long enough in the uncomfortable liminal space, and instead of doing the work of growth we grasp for security and stability too quickly.

All going well, we transform. During the final and third phase, we reintegrate back into our communities. Previously denied parts of ourselves are brought into public view. Like rediscovering old forgotten photographs in a shoebox at the back of a shelf, we find ourselves again. Instead of continuing to hide what we were previously ashamed of, we try to love those parts. We feel content at home on a Saturday night. We let the grey grow through our hair. We stand in crowds unselfconsciously. We say when we're feeling hurt or disappointed. We rest. As Stein says, we take 'the risk of becoming truly oneself'.[12] We return to walking in the mountains.

/

Ngāuruhoe looms against the sky. The track cuts across the mountain's left flank where ancient lava flows have cooled to black jagged fields of rock. Leslie takes the lead and I step in time. Recently, I heard about a study that found if you're walking up a hill with a friend you will judge it as easier than if you walked up the hill by yourself. No one else can walk the hill for me, but walking with another woman makes me feel more able.

We reach a rest stop. Some walkers are taking a break, sitting on their packs to eat a sandwich. Others wait in line at the toilet hut, paper in hand. The air is cooler here than the start of the track. Before us there is a warning sign: 'Consider turning back' it states in yellow lettering. We don't stop, but turn toward the saddle between Tongariro and Ngāuruhoe, which is also known as the Devil's Staircase. It's the crossing's hardest climb, the dusty steps rising to 1600 metres above sea level. We've just been talking about how we both feel scared sometimes. How we feel punch-drunk by this stage of life. And should-we-stop-here-no-let's-keep-going. And our kids and how long it will be until lunch and anxiety and housework and Netflix. And thank fuck we have each other to talk to. 'Here we go,' Leslie says at the first step.

The steps are gruelling. I push my palms against my thighs and lean into the climb. My eyes are fixed on the rocky ground before me: the wooden edge of a step, then rock, then the edge of the next step. My legs ache and my breath burns. *Whose idea was this?* We move in short bursts, powering up a set of steps before stopping to catch our breath. We pass a man and a woman panting to the side of a rise, only to be passed by them minutes later. Everyone moves like this, stopping and starting, working their way up the mountain.

Finally, we step out on to the table plateau of South Crater. It stretches ochre and flat to the horizon. This is where we'll go next. Leslie whoops and slides her pack off her back. She lifts her arms into the air. I bend backwards, my pack sliding to the ground. We both turn to look at where we've come. Below, other people are small bright dots crawling their way up the mountain. How easy the climb looks now we're done; how small the arm of the valley.

/

Reading further, I find that the idea of a three-part transformation is not original to Stein. The line of thought can be traced back through Carl Jung to German scholar Arnold van Gennep, who studied the way different societies use rituals to transition life stages.[13] What van Gennep found was that many rituals have three parts: 'the time before (marked by rites of separation), the time during (marked by rites of transition) and the time after (marked by rites of incorporation).[14] While not every transformation needs an accompanying ritual, rituals provide a comforting container. They help us make sense of what's happening and reassure us that a new normal will eventually be established.[15]

In 1986, Savina Teubal, a Jewish woman living in Los Angeles, created a ritual called 'simchat chochmah' or 'joy of wisdom', which celebrates the wisdom a woman develops during her life and her transition to her elder years. Since its creation, Jewish women entering their seventh or eighth decade have celebrated the simchat chochmah as a way to signal 'their importance in society as holders of wisdom and productive members of the community'.[16] Women withdraw to spend time in study and contemplation, and then take part in a celebration.

While the ritual helped her with personal needs such as facing her own mortality, Teubal says:

> *I created a ceremony, a rite of passage from adult to elder, to establish my presence in the community as a functional and useful human being ... I felt that a crone ceremony filled a significant need in our society.*[17]

The idea of withdrawal reminds me of the first few months of Sam's life. He was born on the floor of our living room after a fast and intense labour. We spent a single night in Wellington Hospital before cocooning ourselves at home, hardly seeing anyone. During that time, I lived by his rhythms, each night a half-dream. I spent hours in the low armchair in his room, feeding or rocking his swaddled body in my arms. I seared with immense love for this tiny creature. I was ferocious and broken with it. During these nights I also contemplated my new, irreversible situation. Waves of panic washed through me. *What have I done? I don't know how to do this!* I thought to myself. *Where has my life gone?* I felt like my old self was dissolving. As a friend put it, I was disassembling to reassemble. While I was officially a mother the moment he was born, a psychological change took place during those quiet months at home. When I stepped back into the world it looked different, and I was a different person.

At the time, I did not see withdrawing with Sam as a life-stage ritual, but it follows the three-step transformation. And while birth seclusion rituals are not formalised in Western society, they are in other cultures such as Nepal, where women rest at a relative's home, or Colombia, where the forty-day *cuarentena* seclusion is traditional.[18, 19] There *are* culturally sanctioned rituals in secular Western society that signal life-stage transitions: the sweet sixteen party; the twenty-first birthday; the university graduation; the wedding; the housewarming; the baby shower; the retirement party; the funeral. Most often these rituals happen over a single day, and focus on celebration, drinking and the giving and receiving of gifts. The measure of a modern wedding is how much money was spent on the bride's dress, or how 'grammable the photos are afterwards, not the space that was created to contemplate marriage itself. Our view is turned out towards the glitter and shine, rather than inwards. I can't help but think that creates an emotional poverty.

And where are the rituals for menstruation, pregnancy and menopause? What does it say about our culture that more fuss is made of retirement from a job than of a woman passing through menopause?[20] And what about women who don't marry, or who are not mothers? Where are the rituals specifically for womanhood that do not relate to these roles? I start nodding in agreement when I read Harald Wydra, a political anthropologist. He writes, 'Despite the skepticism of modern societies towards them, rituals are a vital part of all social communities. They also are crucial to initiate people into new stages of their life.'[21] *Crucial*, he says, because central to all rituals is the shared understanding that we hold something to be sacred. And womanhood is sacred.

One reason I feel that women must create our own rituals is because otherwise we get what the culture gives us. In descriptions of life-stage rituals, the second, liminal phase is associated with feeling invisible. This is because, during this phase, we withdraw from our usual roles and routines. I can't help but notice that the description of this phase echoes the way women describe their experience of midlife. Culturally, we are between young adulthood and old age. I imagine this space as the gloomy bottom of a well. Unlike the protagonist of a 'coming-of-age' story who emerges with new self-possession and freedom, middle-aged women don't emerge. There is no 'coming-of-middle-age' story. Invisibility *becomes* our story.

Years ago, a friend lent me a book about Carl Jung's idea of the 'transcendent function'. Jung proposes that by holding two competing needs in tension without trying to solve the problem, a solution will spontaneously arise from a union between the two. This could be what happens during transition rituals. Jung thought that this process was an activity of the unconscious mind, and it seems to me now that a ritual's purpose is to create a space where the unconscious mind can do its best work.

Walking in the mountains with other women has become one of my rituals for midlife. In Victor Turner's essay on rituals 'Liminality and Communitas', he describes the way people, during transformative rituals, move out of their social roles. We leave behind *lover*, *worker* and *daughter* and enter a space that blends 'lowliness and sacredness'.[22] We get dirty. We get messy. When groups of people share this lowly space, they start to experience a profound togetherness. Life and its order and obligations are suspended for a period of time, and we feel a sense of equality and union with the people around us. There is an absence of social status, property and care about our appearance. In their place come humility and connection. I can't think of a better description of tramping with other women.

I was interested to read Lesley A. Northup, who proposes that rituals primarily for women have a structure that focuses on the 'reassessment, reconfiguration, and development of pre-existing relationships', rather than the classic 'separation, transition, and incorporation' that Stein and other theorists suggest.[23] Northup sees women-specific rituals as 'an enhancement rather than a metamorphosis'[24] and that 'the change wrought by the ritual is toward the interconnectedness of family and friends' rather than 'the hierarchy of social statuses'.[25] I know that seeing and valuing my own interconnectedness helps me recognise my worth and agency. This feels especially important at midlife, as my son grows away from me every day and it won't be long until my parents are gone. It has also made me think about how I can support other women. Whether we are undergoing enhancement or metamorphosis, I think women have a responsibility to make our rituals visible so we can help each other author our lives.

I don't have many rituals of womanhood handed down to me by my mother and grandmother, or the women who came before them. There were many crucial moments in my womanhood that were not seen. I don't know if this emptiness is because my family descends from settlers and I am disconnected from my ancestral homeland. Maybe it is because I grew up in a secular Pākehā family. If anything, the most persistent ritual of my family has been, once or twice a year, to leave everything behind and walk in the mountains.

I wish there had been a ritual for when I started menstruating. I did create one for when I stopped, because, as Germaine Geer writes, midlife needs 'mental preparation and profound acceptance' if it is to be experienced well.[26] This book – and the process of writing – is my way of withdrawing and contemplating what midlife means. It is another of my rituals for midlife. And I am sure that I will find others, because rituals can spontaneously happen. A week after Sam was born I decided to bury his placenta in the garden. I'd asked the midwife to save it for me during the birth because I'd read about other women burying their child's and knew it was an important practice in some cultures. It made sense to me. I couldn't imagine letting the organ that had given him life go into the trash.

It was the middle of winter. Jim dug a hole in the hard ground while I held Sam, both of us wrapped tightly in a wool blanket. My breath ghosted in the air. With one hand, I took photos of Jim pouring the thick fleshy mass from a plastic Tupperware into the hole, before spading the earth back in place. I don't think I said anything special, or anything at all, but I felt the dirt fall as if a part of me were also laid in the hole. A trampoline now floats over the place where the placenta is buried. But I know the spot. I know where that part of my son was returned to the earth.

/

Leslie makes it to Red Crater first, the highest point of the crossing. I struggle up the final slope and stand beside her at the edge. There's nothing between us and a sheer drop into the massive crater mouth. It's impossible to take in the crater's enormity, its dark sweep into the earth. I imagine its moment of creation in the distant past when rocks and lava exploded outward. Steam rises around us in wisps and a sulphurous smell thickens the air. The far face of the crater has sliced away. It ripples down in layers black and rusted red, alien and otherworldly. We stand hushed. I feel my own smallness.

It takes hours to descend the northern slopes of Tongariro. The sky arcs blue above us. We slide foot over foot down volcanic scree. We circle Ngā Rotopounamu, the Emerald Lakes, where minerals turn the water a vibrant green, and Te Wai-whakaata-o-te-Rangihīroa, the Blue Lake. We bound down the track, our arms flung wide for balance, our feet soaring over the ground as we leap across steps and between boulders. In my head I sing: *I am here. I climbed a volcano.* We pass the older sweatbanded women. One has fallen behind; her face looks tired but she's still moving. Her friend waits some distance in front, leg cocked, walking poles hanging from her wrists. Leslie and I fly past. 'That'll soon be us,' I say. 'If we're lucky,' Leslie laughs.

Eventually we reach the long flat hike down to the road end. The track narrows to a thin path enclosed by a canopy of bush. The afternoon sun warms my face. We've been walking for eight hours and we're aching. A young couple runs past us toward track end, their voices loud and joyous. I think about calling my family when we get back. I think of a hot shower and takeaway food. And then, there's the carpark.

/

If you look for them, there are stories of women flourishing and transforming at midlife – but you have to look because it is not the narrative society emphasises. The *Washington Post* article 'Changing Channels' shares the experiences of eight women who achieved personal or professional milestones after the age of fifty. Suzanne Watson, aged fifty-seven, dropped out of medical school in her early twenties to have children, and later, after her husband committed suicide, she raised their four children alone. 'I had never lost the dream to practice medicine. When I was 50, I started to take stock of the years I had left,' Watson says.[27] In her photo she's wearing her white medical coat, her eyes lifted to the sky. She went back to medical school and became a doctor twenty-five years after she was first accepted.

Sandy Warshaw was born into a conservative and religious family, and while she had the opportunity to become a radio producer, the expectation was that she would get married. 'I did what I was supposed to do and married a man … I didn't get to be a disobedient person until much later in life,' Warshaw says.[28] After divorcing, she dated women for sixteen years before finally coming out to her family at age sixty. Patricia Forehand retired from teaching and became a comedian. In one photo she's on stage, microphone in her hand, smiling broadly. 'After I retired, I took the teacher mask off and really cut loose,' she says. 'I do dirty jokes … I feel like I can be myself again.'[29] As a quote attributed to nineteenth-century novelist Mary Ann Evans, who wrote under the penname George Eliot, says, 'It is never too late to be what you might have been.'[30]

While age theorist Margaret Gullette believes we can't eliminate the cultural idea of middle age, she does think that 'with great effort' we can come to see it as 'not inexorably fixed, but subject to … transformation' through telling stories that show midlife as something other than a time of decline.[31] My own story continues to surprise me. Midlife has shown me I can stop grasping for things that I don't really want. I'm learning to forgive other people because I have learned to forgive myself. I think forgiveness is another way of saying we don't need to be perfect. Or, as Maggie Nelson says, 'I am no longer interested in hiding my dependencies in an effort to appear superior to those who are more visibly undone or aching.'[32]

Not long ago I watched *Diane,* a movie about a middle-aged widow living in small-town Massachusetts.[33] Diane, played by Mary Kay Place, is a *doer* and spends most of her day caring for other people. She delivers a casserole to a friend whose husband has had surgery; she volunteers at a local soup kitchen; she plays gin rummy with her cousin Donna, who's in hospital fighting cervical cancer; she brings clean laundry to her son Brian and encourages him to get help for his opiate addiction; she listens to the troubles of her best friend Bobbie while they eat at the local diner. I feel tired watching Diane. She gives every moment to other people and doesn't seem to get any pleasure from her life. Her face is weary and drawn, even when she's with close friends for a meal.

Over a few years, the people in Diane's life stop needing her. Her cousin and best friend die. Her son takes himself to rehab, where he meets his wife. These events send Diane into a period of introspection as she tries to understand her choices. She wanders in the snowy woods. She goes to a bar alone and drunkenly dances to the jukebox. She starts a journal and begins to write poetry. She is haunted by dreams of a summer during her youth when she left her husband and ran away with another man, leaving her son in Donna's care. Diane realises that she's spent her life serving others because she cannot forgive herself for that mistake. She realises she doesn't need to punish herself any more.

I love Diane and her reckoning. I love Diane because I've had to learn to love my own mistakes. One review of *Diane* states that '[i]n the context of the modern multiplex, *Diane* amounts to an act of cinematic bravery' and it is; her story isn't sexy or glamourous.[34] The change in Diane happens in her kitchen and in her bedroom. It happens alone in the woods and in a bar. There's no public spectacle or outburst; no big final speech. It's a subtle change, and her life doesn't look that different afterwards.

Like Diane's, our stories of midlife are often hidden from others. Maybe, one day, there will be a culturally sanctioned ritual for women entering midlife. A time to withdraw and reflect and enjoy the quiet and hilarious company of other woman. But so often we hide our shame. We hide our fear of ageing and change and our uncertainty of what midlife means. I know I do, anyway. But this means we also hide our transformations. We hide the freedom and compassion that comes when we forgive or let go. And we shouldn't. I think of Leslie sitting in the cabin after we arrive back from the tramp. She's talking to her children on the phone – *Yes, a volcano! Yes, I climbed it!* The work may be hardly noticeable from the outside, but that doesn't mean it's not important.

Chapter Seven
The final call

Sheila called me from England before she went into the hospice. From across the world her voice sounded cheerful but also had the low gravelly quality it had developed in her nineties. She told me that my Aunt Sally would be picking her up in a few hours.

We talked a little about the weather. The October days were lengthening as summer came on here in Te Whanganui-a-Tara, whereas the English winter was starting to close in for her. She said that most of the plants in her small garden had been cut back. She hadn't been able to do any gardening for the last few years because of her arthritis and the risk of a fall, so Aunt Sally and Uncle John had done that for her. Maybe the new person moving into her unit will be a gardener, she mused. I asked how she felt about leaving her home, where she had lived for over twenty years, most of it by herself after my grandfather died. 'Oh, I feel fine,' she said. 'I'm ready to go.'

While talking to her I was trying to tidy up the lounge, holding the phone to my ear with one hand while I used the other to pick up books and toys off the floor. Sam was two years old and playing on a rug nearby. Seeing my attention elsewhere, he started to fuss. I gave him a little wave. Slowly his fussing escalated to a cry.

'Go if you need to,' Sheila said. I felt relieved and grateful. She'd had three children herself so she knew I needed to get back to my son. 'I'll give you a call once I'm settled in,' she said, and we made our quick goodbyes. I hung up the phone and walked over and picked up Sam, who immediately stopped crying and wrapped his tiny hand in my hair. My grandmother and I never talked again. She died a week later.

I have thought about that last call many times. Sometimes I feel overcome with shame that I ended the conversation quickly, and that I wasn't giving her my full attention. At other times I think it was the conversation Sheila wanted; she said goodbye without either of us becoming sentimental. Many years earlier when I visited her in England she gave me a pair of delicate silver earrings. As soon as I saw them I knew they were a special gift. Each earring is made up of four circles that intersect to form the petals of a flower. The insides of the petals are finely engraved with a pattern like rays from the sun. She handed me a sealed envelope as I left her house to catch the train to London. 'Wait to open it until you've gone,' she said. When I got on the train I opened the envelope, which held a greeting card. The earrings were sellotaped to the inside beside a note saying that my grandfather had given them to her after he returned from the war. I see our last conversation like that sealed envelope. She didn't want me to open it in front of her, but love was inside.

/

Sheila had been ready to die for some time. She had lost most of her eyesight and could no longer do the small but important things that made her day worthwhile, like a crossword or watching cricket on her television. Over the years her fingers had become so arthritic that she was no longer able to write letters. She had also started to refuse medical treatment for her different ailments. Her lower legs filled with fluid to the point that her ankles vanished. Instead, it appeared as though two small tree trunks rose up from her slippered feet. The swollen skin was taut and bruised, and she had to wear special pressure stockings.

She could also no longer care for her flat, or care for herself at the flat, even with the support of Sally and home help. After my grandfather retired in the late 1980s, my grandparents sold the family home with the pear trees and bought a flat in a retirement complex. The brick units were built in a semicircle around a central green space with a pond (a feature I was always impressed by as a child because it had frogs). Each unit had its own parking space, front door and back garden. Sheila already had the beginnings of arthritis, a disease that runs painfully through my family, and she wanted a smaller house to care for. Both my grandparents wanted to downsize before they had to, and to do so on their own terms. Shortly after the move my grandfather was diagnosed with Parkinson's; the decision had clearly been the right one.

In 2010, a few months before Jim and I got married, I flew to England to visit my grandmother and Sally and John, who lived close by. The week before I arrived, Sheila slipped in the bathroom and broke her leg. Each day, instead of my planned holiday activities, I drove Sally's car along the winding English lanes to the hospital where my grandmother was mending. Once at her ward, I would drag a chair to her bedside and that is where I'd sit until one of the nurses told me visiting hours were over. Our first conversation would always be about what she'd had for breakfast (most mornings, cereal and a glass of apple juice) before she gave me any news of the patients and nurses. There would often be an emergency during the night or some doctor visiting after hours. We covered all of the comings and goings. The ward's low window looked out into a sparsely planted courtyard, and while I listened to her talk, I'd watch birds fly down to ruffle their feathers in the dust. I felt selfish that I enjoyed these days together. The rhythm and repetition, the new closeness. Sheila told me stories about how she'd been a singer and actor as a child, travelling around the West Midlands to do stage shows. She pumped her arms a little and made jazz hands to give me an idea. All of this was news to me.

What I didn't know at the time was the fall that had broken her leg was the first of other falls to come. And that increased falls in elderly people are a sign that their systems are failing and they are moving towards death. After another fall a few months later, Sheila didn't call Sally. Even though she could reach the phone she didn't want to bother anyone. She simply lay on the floor of her flat until my mother happened to ring and then called Sally for help. I think Sheila already felt she was done.

Somehow it didn't occur to me, sitting at Sheila's bedside in the hospital, that she would die soon, even though she was in her nineties. I was still a young woman in my early thirties. I was travelling through Europe before returning home to get married. My grandmother had been there my whole life, a steady presence. A few years earlier her hair had turned bone white. But her face was still rosy. Her eyes were still a luminous blue. Talking to my mother for this book, I realise that the worst of my grandmother's health issues were invisible to me. That was my privilege as her grandchild, but it also meant I wasn't ready for her death. I wasn't thinking about death at all.

/

Soon after Sheila went into hospice she lost consciousness. The hospice nurses called Sally and told her it was time. Sally called my mother and father, who took the first flight they could from Aotearoa to England. When they arrived, jet lagged and worried they'd be too late, they took the two-hour train to Birmingham and then a connecting train to Stourbridge. It's a journey that everyone in my family has made over the years.

John met my parents at the station. It was a cold November afternoon, and mist hung heavily over the tracks and along the grey canal. John drove them to the hospice and they walked through the muted corridors to Sheila's room. She lay in a bed, the covers over her tiny frame. She breathed slowly and her eyes were closed. There were no monitoring machines, so the room was quiet and still. The four of them sat with her for a little while. My mother held her mother's hand. Eventually, John drove everyone back to their cottage for some sleep. Late that evening the call came – Sheila had slipped away.

It's a funny term that, slipped away. Where do we slip to? It is one of the many phrases I've used to avoid stating directly that someone has died. Someone has *passed on* or *lost their battle*. What exactly are we fighting? My family's favourite: *they had a good innings.*

These sayings try to soften the fact that a person we love was here, and now they are not. They have gone from their body, but we do not know to where. These little sayings allow us to sidestep our grief and terror, especially in public, but they also risk us not feeling it in private.

In the last decade of his own life, Philippe Ariès published *Western Attitudes toward Death: From the Middle Ages to the present*, which traces the way our attitudes have changed over time, ending with our modern avoidance of death. Until the Middle Ages, Ariès writes, people lacked a 'modern sense of individualism' so death was seen as a matter of destiny and 'a perfectly natural everyday occurrence'.[1] Death was prepared for and accepted through public rituals, and the rituals surrounding the moment of death were as important as the funeral rites.

From the late Middle Ages, individualism took on a new importance, especially in terms of heavenly judgement. Death became a personal moment of accounting where 'everything was weighed, counted' and a life's failure or success was determined.[2] From the sixteenth century, beliefs about death changed again with the formation of the modern family. During this time, the view of death was sentimental and heightened, with 'ostentatious displays of elaborate funeral ritual and lengthy mourning and memorializing of the deceased'.[3]

What all of these periods have in common is the way people saw death as familiar, natural and everyday – a relationship with death that I don't find in myself. This could be because, from the early twentieth century, death came to be seen as 'ugly and unreal'.[4] People began to avoid talking about death, at first in order to spare the dying person the burden of their own death, but then as a way to avoid 'the overly strong and unbearable emotion caused by the ugliness of dying'.[5] Death became shameful, embarrassing and forbidden and life must always be seen to be happy. I am reminded of the time a therapist told me I cried so quietly that she could hardly tell I was crying at all. As Ariès writes, 'One does not have the right to become emotional other than in private, that is to say, secretly'.[6]

One 2013 study that performed a cross-national comparison of place of death using data from forty-five populations and over 16 million people – more populations than had ever been studied before – found that more than half of deaths occurred in a hospital.[7] Of those who die of cancer, which is the leading cause of death in Aotearoa, only a quarter die at home.[8, 9] I feel wobbly when I read these statistics and Ariès' description of how the moment of death has changed:

Death in the hospital is no longer the occasion of a ritual ceremony, over which the dying person presides amidst his assembled relatives and friends. Death is a technical phenomenon obtained by cessation of care ... Indeed, in the majority of cases the dying person has already lost consciousness.[10]

It seems as though old age and death have gone from being a shared, multi-generational experience to 'something experienced largely alone or with the aid of doctors and institutions'.[11] We shield ourselves from death and pass our shame down the generations.

Another reason we've become strangers to death is that, if we can outsource a loved one's final moment we can also outsource their death rituals. If we don't want to deal with the dead body or the emotions that come with the death of our brother or aunt or wife, we don't have to: the entire dying and funeral process can be managed by someone else. Funerals and cremations have become services to be purchased, just like everything else. This also means death must be made marketable. 'It is not easy to sell something which has no value because it is too familiar and common, or something which is frightening, horrible or painful. In order to sell death, it had to be made friendly', writes Ariès.[12] Cremation is now the preferred funerary rite in England and Aotearoa rather than burial and has also made death more abstract.[13] The person we love becomes a pile of grit in a curved urn. The scattering of ashes can also mean there is no grave site where we can grieve.

When I last went to England, I asked Sally about my grandmother's ashes. We were standing in her sunny cottage kitchen making a pot of tea. I hadn't been able to go to the funeral, I said. Did Grandma have a grave I could visit? I wanted to sit and talk with her for a while. 'She's in the garden shed next to Granddad,' Sally said. As our family lives on opposite sides of the world we hadn't yet found a way to all be together to scatter the ashes. We walked across the neatly cut lawn to the garden shed. It was early morning and the grass was wet with dew. The pale sun filtered through the trees. Sally pulled open the shed door and pointed into the darkness. 'Where?' I asked. I stepped into the narrow space. It smelled like fresh earth and grass clippings. 'There,' she said, and pointed to a low ledge on the back wall. And there they were – two ceramic urns, one slightly larger than the other, tucked in the corner behind a shovel and the mower.

/

When I was in my twenties, a friend of mine killed herself by jumping off a parking building in Te Whanganui-a-Tara. Her funeral was held at a funeral home in Palmerston North, my friend's coffin up on a platform, draped in white silk. When it came time for the eulogy, her mother stood beside the coffin, but instead of talking about my friend she gave a distraught speech about how her ex-husband was her soulmate and her new husband was her soulmate. Both men got onto the platform with her and held her hands. It was strange and unsettling. It was as though her grief for her dead child was unspeakable, so she spoke about something else. At the end of that funeral my friend was wheeled out the back into a hearse, and then everyone left.

The funerals that I have attended have been touching but brief and discreet events. I am given an order of service when I arrive: the mourning schedule. Mourners are moved from one vaulted room to another with precision, so we can mourn as quickly and efficiently as possible. People dab their eyes but no one openly weeps. The eulogies at these funerals list the social, work and academic achievements of the person I love, as though it's essential to recite their curriculum vitae for them to make it through the veil. Afterwards we have a cup of tea and a triangle sandwich.

Even though I have been to a number of such funerals, I have never seen a dead body. The cold, still forms of people I love have always remained hidden beneath the lid of the coffin. I have never even touched a coffin – it has always been on a platform somewhere. I imagine how cool and smooth the wood must feel, the weight if I were to lift one end. The closest I have been to death is when I had my cat Chicken put down. He was fourteen years old and had cancer in the palate of his mouth. The tumour had become big enough that I spotted it one day when he yawned. I should have known. He'd hardly been eating and had become quite thin. His once fluffy orange fur had become tangled and mangy, and little patches were falling out. I just thought he was getting old.

I immediately called the vet and told them about the growth and his thinness, and the nurse asked me when I wanted to bring him in. 'As soon as I can,' I said. 'Today.' 'He could probably last a few more weeks,' the nurse replied, and I felt confused that she'd suggest keeping him alive instead of ending his suffering. Sam was home that day, and while we drove to the vet I explained what would happen to Chicken. That I would hold the cat while the vet gave him an injection, and that the injection would stop his heart. I explained that he wouldn't feel any pain and that I would be there with him. When we arrived I carried Chicken's cage into the examination room. Sam stopped in the waiting room. He looked confused and worried, his forehead crumpled. 'Do you want to stay in the waiting room?' I asked. He nodded, and the vet slid the door closed between us.

I took Chicken out of his cage and placed him on the shiny examination table. The vet looked him over, her gloved hands testing his thinness and opening his jaws. She shook her head. There may have been forms to sign and permissions to give, but I don't remember. When it was time, I picked him up and held him in my lap. 'It's okay, my darling,' I said. He shifted about a bit and then settled in against my legs. I stroked his head. Chicken and I had been together for a long time. He was my friend.

I cupped one hand under his belly as the vet injected him. The room was very quiet. The vet sat down beside me and we watched him become still. Beneath my hands his heartbeat stopped. 'Thank you,' I said. I wrapped his body in a towel. He was limp and heavy and warm. I manoeuvred him back into his cage and then carried him into the waiting room to pay. Sam got up and stood beside me. He looked at the cage and up at my face, and then back at the cage.

I cried on the drive home, giant, body-contorting sobs. 'It's okay,' I said to Sam. 'I'm just really sad because I loved Chicken. It's okay to be really sad,' I said. When we got home I got a spade from the basement and dug a hole in the garden. I was digging and crying and making guttural noises from the bottom of my chest. My hands, face and clothes were covered with wet dirt. When the hole was ready I took Chicken out of his cage and unwrapped him. I wanted to look one last time at this animal who had long been my companion. His body had stiffened and slackened at the same time. His limbs were rigid, but his mouth was hanging to one side, his tongue out. His bladder had emptied onto his fur and the towel. When I lifted him, he was loose. The bright tautness of life was gone.

From a distance, Sam watched me dig. He wasn't sure who this keening and dirty woman was. When I unwrapped Chicken he came over. 'I'm okay,' I reassured him. We went into the house and found an old sewing tin and some scissors. Back in the garden, I cut away a lock of Chicken's orange fur and put it in the tin. 'So we can remember him,' I said to Sam. We wrapped Chicken back in the towel and then in a pillow case, and placed him in the hole. I started to spade dirt onto his body – clods of dark brown on top of white cloth – until there was more dirt than white, and then no whiteness at all.

/

My parents stayed in England for two weeks after Sheila died, which was long enough to go to her funeral. She'd already emptied most of her retirement flat, not wanting to leave the job for her children, but there were still a few items necessary for living that needed to be cleared away. It seemed as though at the end of her life she had taken on the attitude of someone going camping or on a short holiday – you won't be here for long, so you only take what you can carry.

Mum called me on the way to the flat to ask if she could bring me anything of Grandma's. I asked for something personal and everyday. I didn't mind what it was. She brought me home my grandmother's wallet, square and red and with 'London leather goods' stamped on the front. On the inside my grandmother had stuck a Post-it note with Sally's phone numbers and a sticker with her own address. In the pockets were her Sainsbury's card, her B&Q Over Sixties Club Diamond Card, a card for the Dudley Group of Hospitals rheumatology helpline and her Centro concession bus pass. The bus pass had a small photo of Sheila: white hair, polar-fleece jacket, firm eyes.

I am glad to have her wallet. It always sat on the wooden table beside her recliner so she could easily pay the woman who did her hair or the person who cleaned her flat. Whenever I visited, she would reach into the wallet and hand me a ten-pound note, long after I needed the help. 'Take it,' she'd say and pat my hand. The oil from her skin has stained the wallet's magnetic clasp almost black. The leather smells a little of lanolin and hand cream. It's practical and unsentimental, like her.

I keep her wallet in my middle desk drawer. It's got a place in the back corner, out of the way of the scissors, the hole punch and the wrapping paper. Every now and then when the drawer is open Sam sees the wallet and tries to take it out. He's curious. He wants to flip through the pockets and pull out the cards. 'Put it back,' I say gently, and after he does I close the drawer. In these moments, grief is tight in my throat. When my grandmother died I couldn't afford to fly to England. I didn't get to see her in the days before she died or to go to her funeral. But I don't want to cry in front of Sam. To sob and rock and hold my chest for her. So I hide the wallet away.

/

In his book *Being Mortal*, surgeon Atul Gawande writes eloquently about the modern experience of mortality. He argues that we have become detached from the reality of death because modern medicine encourages us to see death as something to be fixed. Gawande tells stories of how doctors fail the dying and their families by focusing almost exclusively on extending life. If death is seen as a medical problem, patients and doctors opt for treatment (often with unbearable side-effects that compromise a person's final few months), rather than creating quality of life and helping people prepare for a good death. 'This is the consequence of a society that faces the final phase of the human life cycle by trying not to think about it,' Gawande writes.[14]

Gawande tells the story of his patient Joseph Lazaroff, who was dying of terminal cancer. Instead of accepting the terminal diagnosis and preparing for the end of his life, he chose to undergo a dangerous surgery to remove the pressure the tumour was putting on his spine. 'It wouldn't cure him, or reverse his paralysis, or get him back to the life he had led,' Gawande writes. 'No matter what we did he had at most a few months to live.'[15] At the time Gawande believed Lazaroff was making the wrong decision.

While the eight-hour operation was a 'technical success', Lazaroff went into respiratory failure and became unconscious.[16] Fourteen days later, his son asked the doctors to stop treatment and let his father die. Gawande was the one to remove his breathing tube. He was struck by how he and other doctors had all avoided talking honestly with Lazaroff. He writes, 'We could never bring ourselves to discuss the larger truth about his condition or the ultimate limits of our capabilities, let alone what might matter most to him as he neared the end of his life. If he was pursuing a delusion, so were we.'[17]

I read Carl Shuker's essay 'In the End' to see whether doctors in Aotearoa also medicalise death or if they focus on a good end of life.[18] I want to know what I'm in for. Shuker argues that while our healthcare spending is similar to the United States (here, too, a quarter of spending goes to the final year of life and most dying people do end up in hospital), that 'less than five per cent' of the care we receive while dying is 'treatment designed to cure'. I am relieved to read that in Aotearoa we seem to give '"good death" supportive care' and not 'invasive medicalised end-of-life care'.[19] Still, Shuker writes, doctors have to learn on the job how to have conversations with dying patients about their mortality and the choices they have. 'Don't we too have that American impulse, with our granny, our dad, our sister, to say, "No, don't you give up; don't ever give up; give us every chance we've got"?' he asks.[20]

In her last years, Sheila developed a blood condition, probably brought on by the radiotherapy treatment she'd received for Hodgkin's disease in the 1980s. The condition meant that every few weeks she needed to go to hospital for a blood transfusion. It was a time-consuming and painful process. A few months before she died, she began to refuse treatment. I guess she had some inner sense that she would die soon, and that she'd rather spend the time left on other things than traipsing down to Dudley Hospital every fortnight.

Will I have the same wisdom? What will I say to my dying parents? Will I try and get them to continue the transfusions or to have the operation? I can understand the desire not to talk about death, either my own or others. My own life feels so bright and immediate that it's strange to imagine one day it will be gone. But more so, I have little practice talking about death. Western society's modern aversion to death has wiped away the tradition and language we once used to help us accept our mortality, and that affects those left behind as much as those who are dying.[21] At a funeral recently, I found myself fumbling my words. In the throng of people I spotted the daughter and granddaughter of my friend who had died, but standing in front of them I felt unsure. A foggy confusion came over me as I tried to offer my condolences.

Maybe this is because I am still getting to know death. In her famous poem 'Because I could not stop for Death – (479)', Emily Dickinson describes death as an inevitable and unhurried presence that makes us 'put away' our striving and lets us appreciate the 'Children', 'the Fields of Gazing Grain' and 'the Setting Sun' – in other words, the rich beauty of our lives.[22] In a series of poems about death, American poet Robert Hass writes about how we experience death at different ages. In 'Those Who Die in Their Twenties' he writes of a friend's suicide, 'Then I thought that his death had a certain glamour, / even though its glamour was despair, which he'd have liked / and probably imagined, and that he shouldn't have.'[23] In 'Harvest: Those Who Die Early in Their Middle Years' Hass writes of his dead friends, 'All of them suddenly become the work / they managed to get done.'[24] The words I remember most are those of Albus Dumbledore, visiting the Hogwarts hospital wing, telling Harry Potter that death is but another adventure.[25] Death, I am finding, is not one thing.

I think Sheila had the death she wanted. She stayed in her own home until a few weeks before she died, supported by Sally, John and carers from community services. She had put aside enough money for her funeral, with a bit left over for each family member. All of her affairs were in order, as they say. She was the one who decided it was time to go into the hospice. Her story ended on her own terms.

But the situation of her death made it difficult for me to make sense of the loss. This is not to criticise my grandmother or my family, but to deeply feel the ways I wasn't able to grieve. I wish I could have been there when she died to say goodbye one last time. I wish I could have gone with Sally and Mum to clear out her flat. Maybe this is how every death feels: we wish for a little more time with the person we've lost. Without these shared experiences, though, the grief feels like a living thing inside me.

On the first anniversary of Sheila's death I planted a flowering daisy in the garden. It has large white flowers with orange centres. It's grown a bit rangy and lopsided but I can see it from the kitchen window. Every anniversary since, I take out her letters and read them. Often, when I'm alone in the study, I take her wallet out of the drawer. I feel the supple leather and put it to my cheek. I pull out the different cards and look at her handwriting, which is curly and formal. I smile at the slightly fed-up expression she has in the photo on her bus card. I open up all of the flaps and the pockets, as though I might find her inside. And in a way I do. 'It's nice to be able to talk about her,' Mum says as we speak on the phone for this book. It is.

/

'Endings matter,' writes Gawande. But the middle matters too. The beliefs we hold about middle age are the children of our beliefs about mortality. If we are embarrassed, uncomfortable and overwhelmed by death, we turn away from its signs. And what greater sign of our own mortality is there than ageing? What are Western beauty standards and youth worship if not a way to avoid admitting that fact? And modern medicine perpetuates the fantasy that we can be ageless.[26] As Ariès writes, 'Technically, we admit that we might die … But really, at heart we feel we are non-mortals.'[27]

Perhaps, but some days I am overwhelmed by grief at my own death. I wake in the middle of the night with fists of panic pounding in my chest. I get out of bed, go into the dim bathroom and run cold water over my hands and wrists. I take slow, full breaths. If the panic is intense I put my thoughts elsewhere by doing addition in lots of thirteen. *Thirteen. Twenty-six. Thirty-nine.* I go into Sam's room, kneel by his bed and stroke his long hair off his face. The night becomes quiet and calm. After a time watching him sleep my finite existence seems okay. Then I go back to bed.

This new panic has arrived because, since entering my forties, death has changed from a vague, gauzy idea to an embodied reality. I remember how it was to feel and look younger, yet now I am not that person. In five years I will be different again. The present moment moves swiftly by and only in one direction. I watch it go. To try and grasp it would be as futile as grasping moving water.

Middles are important because the changes women experience at midlife give us the chance to befriend our mortality. As Darcey Steinke writes of menopause: 'each flash reminds me of my corporeality, my mortality … This is terrifying. It's also a rare opportunity, if faced directly, to come to terms with the limitations of the self.'[28] Middle age is often referred to as the 'sandwich years' to indicate a time when people are caring for both children and elderly parents. Not everyone is a parent, but many of us still have parents. Seeing a parent, a person who was once our entire world, face serious illness or be unable to take care of themselves wakes us up to our own mortality. If they die, we think, then anyone can.

Recently, Mum has started to pare down her possessions and think about which items could be better used elsewhere. When she visits me, she brings me her books. So far, her collection of Janet Frame and most of her feminist texts have ended up on my bookshelf, handed to me a book at a time. A few months ago she turned up with some wool blankets from my childhood. Each time she gives me something, I remind myself of why. Like my grandmother, she knows that clearing out her possessions is an act of love – both the gift of the item, and the gift of her children not having to worry about what to do with it after she's gone. She's slowly preparing to be an elderly woman, which means that I have to prepare for that as well.

About eight months after I started visiting Daphne, she began to lose what she'd come to call our 'friendly matches'. I was winning games, but I wasn't getting any better: Daphne was getting worse. Her memory was failing. She had started to have frequent falls and could no longer push her walker around the house. I would arrive on a Thursday afternoon to find she had been in hospital the day before. She now had carers throughout the day and night because she couldn't get around by herself. One leg was heavily bandaged due to the skin splitting after a fall. I felt terrible for her. On one visit I carried the card table and cards into her sitting room, because she couldn't get out of her chair. 'We can just talk instead of playing a game,' I said. 'No,' she replied, 'these things keep me going.'

There are moments when Daphne reminds me of Sheila. She has the same quick mind and dry sense of humour. She has the same fortitude and dignity. But I am no longer a young woman who avoids old age and death, as I was when I spent time with my grandmother. During one visit Daphne keeps having to wipe saliva from her mouth. I can tell she is frustrated. 'That must be annoying,' I say in a weak attempt at comfort. 'Humiliating,' she corrects. I pause for a moment. The afternoon light from her lounge window flickers over us. It's important to be with what is. To call things what they are. 'Yes,' I say, 'it must be.'

/

Ageing is a privilege that can only be appreciated when it is not feared. And fear is most easily quietened by what we fear becoming familiar. When I tell a friend about how my visits with Daphne have helped me be more comfortable with death, she almost flinches. 'I'm not sure I need that sort of thing in my life,' she says. I understand the desire to turn away, but it doesn't make us any happier.

Gawande writes at length about the work of Laura Carstensen, psychology professor and director of the Stanford Center on Longevity. Carstensen's research found that as people age they report more positive emotions and less depression, anxiety and anger. She believes this is because ageing changes our perspective on how much time we have left in the world, and this in turn helps us focus on what matters the most: the people and relationships in our lives. Carstensen has also found that the same focusing-in effect can be seen in people who've had near-death experiences, such as surviving illness or the 9/11 terrorist attacks. When life starts to feel fragile and finite, 'your focus shifts to the here and now, to everyday pleasures and the people closest to you,' writes Gawande.[29] He suggests that coming to terms with our mortality is a skill we can learn long before old age.[30]

I can only assume that getting cosy with something so threatening and uncomfortable requires regular practice. Anthropologist Anita Hannig, who studies death and dying from a cross-cultural perspective and teaches at Brandeis University in Massachusetts, has created a course to help her students become comfortable with death. Students study bereavement cards, obituaries, kinship death charts, end-of-life wishes, coffins and a range of cultural death practices.[31] 'In order to break through the silence and avoidance that shape … attitudes toward death, we must teach young people different ways to engage with the end of life,' she writes.[32]

Some Buddhists practise *maranasati*, or death awareness meditation, to overcome their fear of death. The practice gives practitioners insight into their impermanence and the reality that 'everything that arises passes away', with the idea that they will then make wiser choices.[33] Practitioners visualise themselves growing old and dying, or those they love dying, and sit with the emotions that arise. 'In Buddhism it is our practice to make ourselves go through the fear of dying now, when many of us are quite young, so that later on it isn't a problem,' writes teacher Larry Rosenberg.[34] '[W]hen marana-sati … is done properly, it's quite astonishing how much stability and peace come out of it,' he says.[35]

Maybe death awareness is what I am practising when I take my grandmother's wallet out of the drawer. When I take a book from my mother's hand. When I look at my face full in the mirror with its new lines and creases, and when I stroke my son's face in the middle of the night. Maybe it's what I am doing when I stand on the edge of a volcano.

/

On Sam's ninth birthday, Jim and I give him a cellphone. He is the first of his friends to get one, and he has agreed to pay for half of the phone and its running costs out of his saved pocket money. I was reluctant to get him a phone so young. I didn't want him to be on social media and none of his friends had phones, so why did he need one? Couldn't he play games on our iPad?

A few weeks before his birthday, we are sitting on our couch talking about the phone. 'I'll be able to call you when I'm at a sleepover,' Sam says. I nod. He makes a good point. The last time he went for a sleepover at his best friend's house I received a call from his friend's father. Sam couldn't sleep, so could I pick him up? Maybe if he'd been able to text me he would have felt more secure and settled. A memory comes back to me of lying on the floor of my friend Holly's bedroom when I was seven years old, unable to sleep, but also too afraid to ask her parents to call mine. 'Okay,' I say, 'but you could take our iPad and message me on that. Wouldn't that work?' Sam scoots closer to me and loops one of his arms through mine. 'If I had a phone I could also message you when I get to school,' he says. We live in a hilly Te Whanganui-a-Tara suburb and the route to school involves crossing a busy road. He's never walked the whole way by himself, and I am nervous for him to try. I look at his open, hopeful face. I make a small *humph* sound. He smiles the smile of victory. 'Then you'd know I was safe,' he says.

The first day he walks to school by himself I drop him just past the first busy road. I get out of the car and give him a hug. 'Text me when you're at school,' I say. I lean against the car and watch him run down the road, his legs wheeling outwards and his long hair flopping against his bag. He turns and swings one hand into the air. 'Bye!' he yells. It's early spring. The sky that morning is clear blue above the hill line. I am reminded of something Robert Pogue Harrison wrote about ageing:

> The sky I see today is more or less the same blue spectacle it always was, yet it's not the same sky of old. When I was seven it was my body's covenant with the cosmos; by twenty it became the face of an abstraction; today it's the dome of a house I know I will not inhabit for too much longer; shortly it will be the answer to what today still remains a question.[36]

I do not know how long I will live under this domed sky. One day quite soon I will be holding some everyday object of my mother's. I will place it in the drawer beside the red wallet. Soon after, relatively speaking, my son will hold something of my own. It is hard to be present at someone else's death, but it's harder to be with our own slow dying. It's important to be with what is. He's almost gone – a flash of school backpack around the corner. I turn towards home.

Afterword

When my father first came out as transgender I felt both grief and anger. In part that was because I found out by accident instead of my parents sitting me down to tell me. Jim's parents had travelled from England and we were taking them to meet mine for the first time. We'd taken the ferry from Te Whanganui-a-Tara across to Waitohi Picton, and then driven down the rolling Kaikōura coast to Ōtautahi, where my parents live. We were staying with them for a few days.

After breakfast on the first morning I went into my parents' study to use their computer. I wanted to look at some of the holiday snaps we'd taken the week before and that I'd uploaded to the website Flickr. As I went to type in the website's address, the browser auto-filled. I assumed it was from the last time I'd stayed with my parents so I hit enter. The screen filled with images of a smartly dressed older woman. In one image she was wearing a floral dress and standing in my parents' garden. In another she wore a pink blazer buttoned over a blouse and a pencil skirt, and what appeared to be a wig of long platinum hair. Feet together, her hands interlaced in front of her, she appeared shy. Dad looked so much like her own mother that it took a few moments to realise what I was seeing.

Immediately I found Mum in the kitchen where she was making everyone morning tea. In a whisper, I told her what I had seen on the computer. At first she was angry, her face flushed – how dare I snoop, it's none of my business – but then she started to cry. She leaned against me. 'I'm so glad I can finally tell you,' she said.

At the time I couldn't make sense of why my parents kept Dad's gender a secret. I had close friends who'd transitioned or who were gender non-conforming. I am part of the LGBTQIA+ community. It's obvious to me now that my father's secrecy was more to do with her fear and shame than anything to do with me. But still, the night after I found out, I didn't feel acceptance. I lay in bed beside my sleeping husband as the swells and currents of grief ripped through me. I couldn't fall asleep until the early hours of the morning. A few months later, I introduced my father to some friends at a book event in Ōtautahi. She turned to me angrily and said, 'Don't call me Dad.' I felt as though my father had died.

I also felt angry. My father and I have always had a tricky relationship – we're too much like each other – but now I felt she was claiming womanhood without any lived experience. I was angry that she'd spent her life working as a White, male, cisgender academic with the status and professional rewards that gave her. I was angry that she had benefited from traditional gender roles in our family. It was my mother who had cooked every evening meal of my childhood and who had cared for the emotional lives of my sister and me. And now the children had left and that labour was done, my father was a woman? I was angry that my relationship with my body was influenced by how my father had valued women's bodies for their thinness and tautness, for their blondeness and youth, and that after coming out she expressed and valued her own womanhood that way.

It took a few years for me to realise that my father never lived her life as a man, but as a closeted transgender woman. This fact is obvious now when I write it. My sister and I would often find her wigs hidden in the back of the hallway cupboard as we searched for the Christmas presents our mother would stash. We'd turn the blonde bundles over in our hands and ask each other, *Was Mum losing her hair? Was it some* sex *thing?* It never occurred to us that the wigs might belong to the fishing, tramping, gold-mining-obsessed geography lecturer that was our dad. To the person who dressed in old t-shirts, blue stubbies and walking socks pulled up to mid-calf. After coming out, Dad revealed that she'd spent years in a secret binge-and-purge cycle – dressing in women's clothing while the family was out during the day, and then being so gripped by shame and disgust that she would burn everything in the large steel drum we used for rubbish. My father *did* have a lived experience of womanhood, and it was one totally different to my own.

Writing this book has shown me that I don't need to hold on so tightly to my womanhood. I don't need to defend it from other experiences of womanhood, or to change myself to fit a particular definition of womanhood. I can let it be different things. I can let it be loose and beautiful and contradictory and pleasurable and complex.

The first two decades of the twenty-first century have seen huge cultural shifts in the ways we understand gender. The recognition of genders outside the binary didn't happen organically, but came about because of concerted pressure from LGBTQIA+ rights activists. In 2011, the Tumblr site Ask a Non-Binary began answering reader's questions. In 2014, Facebook announced they would be adding a new field where transgender and gender non-conforming people could identify their gender.[1] The same year, actor Laverne Cox appeared on the cover of *Time* magazine with the heading 'The

Transgender Tipping Point: America's next civil rights frontier'.[2] In 2017, *Scientific American* published a graphic called 'Beyond XX and XY'.[3] The double-page spread shows the multiple factors that influence the broad, non-binary spectrum of biological sex, as well as how biological sex is separate from the spectrums for gender and sexuality. In January 2020, the American Dialect Society voted the singular pronoun 'they' the most important word in the last decade.[4] As queer activist Jacob Tobia said, 'By now, the cultural visibility of the transgender, genderqueer and gender nonconforming community has seriously expanded the way that we view gender.'[5]

I can see Sam has a different understanding of gender to mine at his age. He doesn't assume another child is a girl because of their clothing or hair. He sees his own gender as something he'll continue to discover as he grows older. At the moment he identifies as a boy. He wears his hair long and paints his nails in rainbow colours. Sometimes he likes to shave his legs. There's space for him to explore his gender expression where there wasn't for me. The other day he tipped his head to one side and said, 'I'll probably be a boy when I grow up, but I haven't figured it out yet.'

The move away from the gender binary is as important for women as it is for people who are gender diverse, because the norms that exclude and promote violence against trans and gender non-conforming people are the same ones that constrict and diminish womanhood. A gender-diverse world cannot be created by simply adding a non-binary gender to the existing binary. That is because the gender binary is a closed system that requires the two parts – men and women – to be in opposition to each other. Men are strong; women are weak. Men are rational; women are emotional. Men are capable; women are hysterical. These narrow gender norms take us further away from ourselves and each other, but by dismantling the gender binary we free everyone.

It's a rainy summer afternoon and I'm talking to Nikki on the phone. I am working through the final edits on the book. I've phoned to check that she's okay with me calling her 'Dad' and 'my father' alongside 'Nikki' and 'she'. 'I can change it to whatever you want,' I say. She's just come back from having coffee at the local café with Mum. She tells me that she doesn't mind. While she used to get upset by the term 'Dad', she's okay with it now. 'It's a biological reality. I've mellowed,' she says.

We talk about how she still sometimes presents as male, just to make life easier. She does this when she's with her gold-mining friends ('They can't understand') and when she publishes academic papers. She tells me she presented as male a few years ago when she needed chemo for prostate cancer. 'Otherwise it would have been too complicated,' she says. We sit in silence for a moment. 'I sometimes present as male for your mum,' she says. I ask if she finds that hard or if it causes her gender dysphoria. 'I don't mind. She didn't sign up to be married to a woman,' she says. Then Dad pauses. 'If I'd come out when I was thirty, things might have been different.' These conversations help close the space between us. Later, her words still held in my chest, I remember a passage from *The Argonauts*: 'How to explain, in a culture frantic for resolution, that sometimes the shit stays messy?'[6]

In the end, 'What does it mean to be a woman?' is a flawed question. It presumes a single answer or experience, or that there should be one. My own womanhood is an alchemy of both my mother's and my father's womanhood. It's a kaleidoscope of culture and friendship and sex and marriage and motherhood and blood and language and a walnut walking stick and a maroon velvet dress. It is a uterus and the space of no-uterus.

Women, throughout our lives, and as society pushes forward, will have to constantly remake our identities and ideas of womanhood.

If there's anything the women around me are good at, it's rebuilding themselves, and I cannot see that as anything but a gift. But how do we stop reducing ourselves, carving our bodies away until we're bone? How do we value the messy, hidden women inside? I can only think it's from a place where gender does not tell our complete story.

Acknowledgements

Some of the chapters of this book have appeared as abridged versions in *The Pantograph Punch, Strong Words #2: The Best of the Landfall Essay Competition* (Otago University Press, 2021) and *Action, Spectacle*. Thank you to the editors of those publications.

Grateful acknowledgement is made to all of the authors, publishers and literary representatives who gave permission to quote from copyright material. Material from *Western Attitudes toward Death: From the Middle Ages to the present* by Philippe Ariès, trans. Patricia M. Ranum (pp. 87, 88, 89, 99, 105, 106), © 1974 Johns Hopkins University Press, used by permission of Johns Hopkins University Press; material from *Why I'm No Longer Talking to White People About Race* by Reni Eddo-Lodge, © Reni Eddo-Lodge, 2018, Bloomsbury Publishing Plc, used by permission of Bloomsbury Publishing Plc.; quotations from 'Māori Women: Caught in the contradiction of a colonised reality' by Annie Mikaere, originally published in *Waikato Law Review*, vol. 2, 1994, used by permission of Waikato Law Review; material from *Flash Count Diary: A new story about menopause* by Darcey Steinke, © Darcey Steinke, 2019, used by permission of Cannongate Books; material from *Beyond the Gender Binary* by Alok Vaid-Menon used by permission of Penguin Young Readers Group, a division of Penguin Random House LLC, all rights reserved.

My first thanks must go to my parents Pauline Barnett and Nikki Smith for the grace and generosity they have shown in allowing me to write about them in this book. It's an act of pure love because this book only gives my side of the story, and yet families are made up of multiple perspectives. I am grateful to them for their support and proud to be their daughter.

Gratitude and thanks to my amazing publisher Sue Wootton for her belief in this book. Thank you also to the team at Otago University Press for their hard work on the book, especially designer Fiona Moffat for the cover and editor Anna Hodge for bringing her smart, thorough and kind editing eye to my work. Thank you to Pip Adam, Hinemoana Baker (Ngāti Raukawa, Ngāti Toa Rangatira, Te Āti Awa and Ngāi Tahu), Lynn Jenner, Kirsten McDougall and Bryan Walpert, all of whom read sections or the entirety of this book and gave me insightful feedback and warm encouragement. I appreciate their time and mahi in helping me make this book much better than I could have done alone. Thank you also to my brilliant writers' group for sharing our writing lives over these many years, and for feedback on early chapters, especially Alison Glenny, Rachel O'Neill, Lawrence Patchett, Tina Makereti (Ngāti Tūwharetoa, Te Ati Awa, Ngāti Rangatahi), Bill Nelson and John Summers (Pip Adam and Lynn Jenner are also part of this group). Thank you to Diane McIndoe for her support and wisdom, to Daphne for our games and conversations and to Age Concern Wellington. A special thank you to Henrietta Harris and Melanie Roger Gallery for permission to use Henrietta's painting *Fixed It XVI* on the cover. A huge thank you and much love to the friends who I mention in this book for generously allowing me to share their stories: Kristina Kirk, Rhiannon Newcombe, Kirsten McDougall, Melissa Fear, Leslie Titheridge, Nicola Melville and Helen Lehndorf, and to the special people who just deserve to be mentioned: my sister Jen Barnett, Megan Hinge, Tim Wright and Sarah Blaschke.

Thank you to Creative New Zealand for an arts grant that came at the perfect time. Without that money the book would not have been finished.

Thank you to my dear husband Jim and our son Sam for your constant support and encouragement. You are my greatest teachers of love and humility. You are the unwavering stars in my night sky.

The biggest thank you is to the feminists and LGBTQIA+ activists, creators and teachers who have written, protested, picketed, podcasted, petitioned, stood up, spoken up, made art, made speeches, made movies, made relationships, made change and who didn't give up advocating for freedom from discrimination. They have done (and are still doing) the work of social change and share it generously with the world. While many of these people are household names, most are living or did live ordinary heroic lives. As I am a cisgender Pākehā woman, there is little physical or social threat in me questioning and being curious about my gender and its relationship with systems of power. This has not been the case for many women and LGBTQIA+ people throughout history and today, and especially people of colour. I am in their debt.

Notes

Page 5

The Eve Fairbanks quote came from her piece '"We believed we could remake ourselves any way we liked": how the 1990s shaped #MeToo', which appeared in *The Guardian*, 5 July 2018.

The lines of poetry by Hinemoana Baker are from 'If I Had to Sing', which appears in the collection *Funkhaus* (Wellington: Victoria University Press, 2020), p.15.

Works not cited

There are two books that heavily influenced my thinking and the content of this book, but that I did not end up citing. They are *Rage Becomes Her: The power of women's anger* (New York: Atria Books, 2018) by Soraya Chemaly, which illuminates why women repress rage and the damage that does, and the way our rage can be a tool for personal and political change. Chemaly's book is also an excellent resource on the added discrimination faced by women of colour. The other is *Wild: From lost to found on the Pacific Crest Trail* (New York: Alfred A. Knopf, 2012), Cheryl Strayed's memoir about how the experience of suddenly losing her mother to cancer plunged her into years of grief, heroin use and multiple affairs that eventually ended her marriage. At twenty-six, and with no hiking experience, Strayed made a decision to walk one of the longest trails in the United States, the Pacific Crest Trail. Over three months, she walked 1100 miles alone in the wilderness – through the Mojave Desert, California and Oregon, eventually finishing in Washington State. The process of walking allowed Strayed to forgive herself. 'Hiking the PCT', she writes, 'was my way back to the person I used to be'.

Chapter One: Women without a uterus

1. Chidera Eggerue, 'Saggy Boobs Matter', The Slumflower blog: www.theslumflower.com/blog/saggy-boobs. Eggerue has since taken down her blog but has two books: *What a Time To Be Alone: The slumflower's guide to why you are already enough* (London: Quadrille Publishing Ltd, 2018) and *How To Get Over a Boy*, (London: Quadrille Publishing Ltd, 2020).
2. Ivan E. Coyote, *Tomboy Survival Guide* (Vancouver: Arsenal Pulp Press, 2018), p. 14.
3. Ibid., p. 13.
4. Eve Fairbanks, '"We believed we could remake ourselves any way we liked": How the 1990s shaped #MeToo', *The Guardian*, 5 July 2018, para. 6: www.theguardian.com/news/2018/jul/05/we-believed-we-could-remake-ourselves-any-way-we-liked-how-the-1990s-shaped-metoo

5. Ibid., para. 8.

6. Ibid., para. 21.

7. Ibid., para. 48.

8. Jessica Eaton, 'Why I don't want women to become "equal to men"', *Victim Focus*, 4 August 2018, para. 6: https://victimfocus.wordpress.com/2018/08/04/why-i-I-want-to-become-equal-to-men

9. Hannah Gadsby, *Nanette*, directed by Jon Olb and Madeleine Parry, Netflix, 19 June 2018: www.netflix.com/watch/80233611

10. Meera Atkinson, 'Patriarchy perpetuates trauma. It's time to face the fact', *The Guardian*, 30 April 2018, para. 2: www.theguardian.com/commentisfree/2018/apr/30/patriarchy-perpetuates-trauma-its-time-to-face-the-fact

11. Ibid., para. 4.

12. Natalie Wynn, 'Beauty', *ContraPoints*, 22 May 2019: www.youtube.com/watch?v=n9mspMJTNEY

13. Alok Vaid-Menon, *Beyond the Gender Binary* (New York: Penguin Workshop, 2020), pp. 29–30.

14. Maggie Nelson, *The Argonauts* (Melbourne, Australia: Text Publishing, 2015), p. 64.

15. Claudia Dey, 'Mothers as Makers of Death', *The Paris Review*, 14 August 2018, para. 8: www.theparisreview.org/blog/2018/08/14/mothers-as-makers-of-death

Chapter Two: I miss your pussy

1. Robert Pogue Harrison, *Juvenescence: A cultural history of our age* (Chicago and London: University of Chicago Press, 2014), p. x.

2. Figure based on an average of statistics from: www.parliament.nz/en/pb/research-papers/document/00PlibCIP181/household-incomes-inequality-and-poverty; www.stats.govt.nz/news/child-poverty-statistics-released

3. Harrison, *Juvenescence*, p. x.

4. Anthony Browne, 'The obsession with eternal youth', *The Guardian*, 7 April 2002, para. 18: www.theguardian.com/education/2002/apr/07/medicalscience.highereducation

5. Margaret Morganroth Gullette, 'Midlife Discourses in the Twentieth-Century United States: An essay on the sexuality, ideology, and politics of "Middle Ageism"', in *Welcome to Middle Age! (and other cultural fictions)*, ed. Richard Shweder (Chicago: University of Chicago Press, 1998), p. 18.

6. Megan Jayne Crabbe, *Body Positive Power: How to stop dieting, make peace with your body and live* (London: Ebury Digital, 2017), p. 23.

7. Gullette, 'Midlife Discourses', p. 14.

8. Amara Lindsay Miller, 'Eating the Other Yogi: Kathryn Budig, the yoga industrial complex, and the appropriation of body positivity', *Race and Yoga*, vol. 1, no. 1, 2016, p. 12: https://escholarship.org/uc/item/2t4362b9

9. Ibid.

10. Naomi Wolf, *The Beauty Myth: How images of beauty are used against women* (New York: HarperCollins, 2002), p. 14.

11. Ibid., p. 8.

12. Ibid.

13. Naomi Wolf, *The Beauty Myth: How images of beauty are used against women* (London: Vintage Books, 2015), p. xi.

14. Rebecca Onion, 'A Modern Feminist Classic Changed My Life. Was It Actually Garbage?' *Slate*, 30 March

2021: https://slate.com/human-interest/2021/03/naomi-wolf-beauty-myth-feminism-conspiracy-theories.html

15. Ibid., para. 6.

16. Ibid.

17. Ibid., para. 8.

18. Miller, 'Eating the Other Yogi', p. 4.

19. Jasper Jackson, 'Sadiq Khan moves to ban body-shaming ads from London transport', *The Guardian*, 13 June 2016, para. 6: www.theguardian.com/media/2016/jun/13/sadiq-khan-moves-to-ban-body-shaming-ads-from-london-transport

20. Isabelle Fol, *The Dominance of the Male Gaze in Hollywood Films: Patriarchal Hollywood images of women at the turn of the millennium* (Norderstedt, Germany: Diplomarbeiten Agentur Diplom.de, 2004), p. 2.

21. Suzanna D. Walters, *Material Girls: Making sense of feminist cultural theory* (Berkeley and Los Angeles, California: University of California Press, 1995), p. 58.

22. Fol, *Dominance of the Male Gaze*, p. 5.

23. John Berger, *Ways of Seeing* (London: British Broadcasting Corporation and Penguin Books, 1972), p. 47.

24. Mary Devereaux, quoted in Walters, *Material Girls*, p. 57.

25. Berger, *Ways of Seeing*, p. 47.

26. Akiko Busch, 'The Invisibility of Older Women', *The Atlantic*, 28 February 2019, para. 6: www.theatlantic.com/entertainment/archive/2019/02/akiko-busch-mrs-dalloway-shows-aging-has-benefits/583480/

27. Sara M. Hofmeier, Cristin D. Runfola, Margarita Sala, Danielle A. Gagne, Kimberly A. Brownley

and Cynthia M. Bulik, 'Body Image, Aging, and Identity in Women over 50: The Gender and Body Image (GABI) study', *Journal of Women & Aging*, vol. 29, no. 1, 2017, para. 2, doi: 10.1080/08952841.2015.1065140

28. Ibid., para. 29.

29. Ibid., para. 28.

30. Dorthe Nors, 'On the invisibility of middle-aged women', *Literary Hub*, 22 June 2016, para. 7: https://lithub.com/on-the-invisibility-of-middle-aged-women

31. Ministry for Women and Statistics New Zealand, *Effect of Motherhood on Pay – methodology and full results June 2016 quarter* (Wellington, New Zealand: Statistics New Zealand, 2017), p. 10: www.stats.govt.nz/assets/Reports/Effect-of-motherhood-on-pay-methodology-and-full-results/effect-of-motherhood-on-pay-methodology-full-results.pdf. This report states that while parents earn more than non-parents, there is a 'significantly larger pay gap between male parents and female parents than there is between male non-parents and female non-parents', which is called the 'motherhood penalty'.

Chapter Three: Making gender trouble

1. Judith Butler, *Gender Trouble: Feminism and the subversion of identity* (New York and London: Routledge/Taylor and Francis e-Library, 2002), p. 43.

2. Ibid.

3. Ibid.

4. Wikipedia, 'Femininity', para. 2: https://en.wikipedia.org/wiki/Femininity

5. Liz Kotz, 'The Body You Want: An interview with Judith Butler', *Art Forum Magazine*, vol. 31, no. 3, November 1992, para. 13: www.artforum.com/print/199209/the-body-you-want-an-inteview-with-judith-butler-33505

6. Butler, quoted in Kotz, 'The Body You Want', para. 17.

7. Maggie Nelson, *The Argonauts* (Melbourne, Australia: Text Publishing, 2015), p. 122.

8. Poppy Marriott and Tom Rasmussen, 'Vibrant Colors, Buzzcuts, & Freedom: This is non-binary hair in all its glory', *Refinery29*, 4 May 2019, para. 12: www.refinery29.com/en-us/non-binary-hairstyles-hair-color

9. Ibid.

10. Butler, *Gender Trouble*, p. xi.

11. Ibid., p. 9. Butler specifically uses this phrase to refer to heteronormativity, but throughout *Gender Trouble* refers to the coherence and stability of gender norms within 'the binary gender system' (p. 30), so here I have used it more generally.

12. Ibid., p. xii. Butler refers to it as both 'policing gender' and 'gender policing', which has become the colloquial term.

13. Sharan Dhaliwal, 'These Intimate Portraits Examine How Hair Connects to Gender Identity', *Vice*, 26 October 2018, para. 3: www.vice.com/en_us/article/yw983m/hair-portraits-gender-identity-women

14. Ibid., para. 2.

15. Ibid., para. 4.

16. The statistics were drawn from two pages – Human Rights Campaign, 'A National Epidemic: Fatal anti-transgender violence in America in 2018': www.hrc.org/resources/a-national-epidemic-fatal-anti-transgender-violence-in-america-in-2018; and Human Rights Campaign, 'A National Epidemic: Fatal anti-transgender violence in the United States in 2019': www.hrc.org/resources/a-national-epidemic-fatal-anti-trans-violence-in-the-united-states-in-2019

17. Human Rights Campaign, 'Fatal Violence Against the Transgender and Gender Non-Conforming Community in 2020': www.hrc.org/resources/violence-against-the-trans-and-gender-non-conforming-community-in-2020

18. Alok Vaid-Menon, *Beyond the Gender Binary* (New York: Penguin Workshop, 2020), pp. 27–28.

19. Christian Reighter, 'I don't want children – stop telling me I'll change my mind', TED: Ideas worth spreading, October 2016: www.ted.com/talks/christen_reighter_i_don_t_want_children_stop_telling_me_i_ll_change_my_mind

20. Ibid., 12.00 min. (in English transcript).

21. Ibid., 13.17 min. (in English transcript).

22. Butler, *Gender Trouble*, p. 189.

23. Darcey Steinke, *Flash Count Diary: A new story about the menopause* (Edinburgh: Canongate Books, 2019), p. 81.

24. Ibid.

25. Ibid., p. 13.

26. Ibid., pp. 30–31.

27. Ibid., p. 188.

28. Ibid., p. 191.

29. Ibid., pp. 193–4.

30. Ibid., p. 191.

31. Kittisaro, '#214: The Case for Devotion, Kittisaro and Thanissara', interview by

Dan Harris, *Ten Percent Happier with Dan Harris*, 20 November 2019, 1 hour 31.30 min.: www.tenpercent.com/ten-percent-happier-podcast

32. Steinke, *Flash Count Diary*, p. 90.
33. Ibid., p. 93.

Chapter Four: Genealogy of care

1. Holly Walker, *The Whole Intimate Mess: Motherhood, politics, and women's writing* (Wellington: Bridget Williams Books, 2017), pp. 76–81.
2. Lynn Steger Strong, 'A dirty secret: you can only be a writer if you can afford it', *The Guardian*, 27 February 2020, para. 9: www.theguardian.com/us-news/2020/feb/27/a-dirty-secret-you-can-only-be-a-writer-if-you-can-afford-it
3. Barbara Brookes, Jane McCabe and Angela Wanhalla (eds), *Past Caring? Women, work and emotion* (Dunedin: Otago University Press, 2019), p. 18. The term 'shadow labour' was coined by social critic Ivan Illich.
4. Hugh Armstrong and Pat Armstrong, *Thinking It Through: Women, work and caring in the new millennium* (Halifax: Healthy Balance Research Program, 2002), p. 4: https://cdn.dal.ca/content/elissalusie/pdf/diff/ace-womenhealth/Healthy%20Balance/ACEWH_hbrp_thinking_it_through_women_work_caring_new_millennium.pdf
5. Brookes et al., *Past Caring?*, p. 30.
6. Prue Hyman, *Hopes Dashed? The economics of gender inequality* (Wellington: Bridget Williams Books, 2017), p. 23. Hyman reports that the results of the later 2009–10 time use survey were very similar.
7. Brookes et al., *Past Caring?*, p. 21.

8. Hyman, *Hopes Dashed?*, p. 44.
9. Brookes et al., *Past Caring?*, p. 31.
10. Ibid., p. 20.
11. Ibid.
12. Ibid., p. 28.
13. Ibid.
14. Ibid., p. 32.
15. Keryn O'Neill and Sue Younger, 'Our Literature Search into Childcare: How are the children doing?', Brainwave Trust Aotearoa, 2016: https://brainwave.org.nz/article/our-literature-search-into-childcare-how-are-the-children-doing
16. Megan K. Maas, 'How toys became gendered – and why it'll take more than a gender-neutral doll to change how boys perceive femininity', *The Conversation*, 5 December 2019, para. 19: https://theconversation.com/how-toys-became-gendered-and-why-itll-take-more-than-a-gender-neutral-doll-to-change-how-boys-perceive-femininity-124386
17. Patrick Huguenin, 'Women really click with The Sims', *Daily News*, 15 April 2008, para. 3: www.nydailynews.com/life-style/women-click-sims-article-1.283191
18. Jane McCabe, 'In the Darkness of Night: Traversing worlds through the concept of ayah care', in Brookes et al., *Past Caring?*, p. 99.
19. Emma, 'The gender wars of household chores: A feminist comic', *The Guardian*, 26 May 2017: www.theguardian.com/world/2017/may/26/gender-wars-household-chores-comic
20. Ibid.
21. This quote is widely attributed to American writer Jim Loehr. It appears be a paraphrase of William James: 'My

experience is what I agree to attend to', *The Principles of Psychology*, vol. 1, 1890.

22. Nicole LePera (@the.holistic. psychologist), 'Thank you mom for bringing me into the cycle. It forced me to find a way out + forgive both of us #selfhealers', Instagram, 21 April 2020: www.instagram.com/p/B_ NdWt6gg-R

23. Meagan Tyler, 'No, feminism is not about choice', *The Conversation*, 30 April 2015: https://theconversation.com/no-feminism-is-not-about-choice-40896

24. Belinda A.E. Borell, Amanda S. Gregory, Tim N. McCreanor, Victoria G.L. Jensen and Helen E. Moewaka Barnes, 'It's Hard at the Top but it's a Whole Lot Easier than Being at the Bottom: The role of privilege in understanding disparities in Aotearoa/New Zealand', *Race/Ethnicity Multidisciplinary Global Contexts*, vol. 3, no. 1, 2009, p. 33.

25. Analytics and Insights team, The Treasury, *Statistical Analysis of Ethnic Wage Gaps in New Zealand: Analytical Paper 18/03*, September 2018, 'Table 2: Mean ethnic group hourly wages and their ratios: HLFS June quarters 2016–17', p. 6: www.treasury.govt.nz/sites/default/files/2018-08/ap18-03.pdf

26. Ibid., p. 9.

27. Hyman, *Hopes Dashed?*, p. 34.

28. Ministry of Women, 'Wāhine Māori', para. 2: https://women.govt.nz/w%C4%81hine-m%C4%81ori

29. Ministry of Health, 'Socioeconomic indicators': www.health.govt.nz/our-work/populations/maori-health/tatau-kahukura-maori-health-statistics/nga-awe-o-te-hauora-socioeconomic-determinants-health/socioeconomic-indicators#1

30. Julia Amua Whaipooti, 'Minneapolis has vowed to defund its police. New Zealand needs to have that conversation', *The Guardian*, 10 June 2020, para. 8: www.theguardian.com/world/2020/junelissalisolis-has-vowed-to-defund-its-police-new-zealand-needs-to-have-that-conversation

31. Annie Mikaere, 'Māori Women: Caught in the contradiction of a colonised reality', *Waikato Law Review*, vol. 2, 1994, paras 5–6: www.waikato.ac.nz/law/research/waikato_law_review/pubs/volume_2_1994/7

32. Ibid., para. 2.

33. Ibid., para. 9.

34. Ibid., para. 15.

35. Ibid.

36. Ibid., para. 16.

37. Reni Eddo-Lodge, *Why I'm No Longer Talking To White People About Race* (London: Bloomsbury, 2018), p. 149.

38. Maggie Nelson, *The Argonauts* (Melbourne, Australia: Text Publishing, 2015), p. 121.

39. Teresa Cowie, 'What Pasifika families' unpaid work means to New Zealand', Radio New Zealand, 10 September 2020, para. 6: www.rnz.co.nz/news/in-depth/425685/what-pasifika-families-unpaid-work-means-to-new-zealand

40. Seini Taufa, quoted in Cowie, 'Pasifika families' unpaid work', para. 7.

41. Eddo-Lodge, *No Longer Talking*, p. 181.

42. Max Harris, 'Racism and White Defensiveness in Aotearoa: A Pākehā perspective', *E-Tangata*, 10 June 2018, para. 29: https://e-tangata.co.nz/comment-and-analysis/racism-and-white-defensiveness-in-aotearoa-a-pakeha-perspective

43. Ibid., para. 10.

44. Borell et al., 'Hard at the Top', p. 33.
45. Ibid., p. 31.
46. Strong, 'A dirty secret', para. 9.
47. Makanaka Tuwe, 'Projectile Solidarity', *The Pantograph Punch*, 7 June 2021: https://pantograph-punch.com/posts/projectile-solidarity?
48. Tuwe, 'Projectile Solidarity', paras 5 and 17.

Chapter Five: Grotesque bodies

1. Richard A. Shweder, 'Preface', in *Welcome to Middle Age! (and other cultural fictions)*, ed. Richard Shweder (Chicago: University of Chicago Press, 1998), p. vii.
2. Richard A. Shweder, 'Introduction: Welcome to Middle Age!' in Shweder, *Welcome to Middle Age!*, p. x.
3. Margaret Morganroth Gullette, 'Midlife Discourses in the Twentieth-Century United States: An essay on the sexuality, ideology, and politics of "Middle Ageism"', in Shweder, *Welcome to Middle Age!*, p. 17.
4. Margaret Lock, 'Deconstructing the Change: Female maturation in Japan and North America', in Shweder, *Welcome to Middle Age!*, p. 45.
5. Ibid., p. 48.
6. 'Behind Closed Doors', *Meet the Romans with Mary Beard*, episode 3, directed by Hugo MacGregor, Lion Television A113 Media and BBC, 2012, 24.30 min.
7. William A. Fischel, *Making the Grade: The economic evolution of American school districts* (Chicago: University of Chicago Press, 2009), p. 79. Fischel notes that age grading was preceded by ability grading, where children of similar abilities were taught together despite age.
8. Ibid., p. 80.
9. Ibid., p. 82.
10. David Foster Wallace, 'Plain old untrendy troubles and emotions', *The Guardian*, 20 September 2008: www.theguardian.com/books/2008/sep/20/fiction
11. Gullette, 'Midlife Discourses', p. 23.
12. Bradd A. Shore, 'Status Reversal: The coming of aging in Samoa', in Shweder, *Welcome to Middle Age!*, p. 105.
13. Gullette, 'Midlife Discourses', p. 23.
14. Ibid., p. 24.
15. Germaine Greer, *The Change: Women, ageing and the menopause* (London: Hamish Hamilton, 1991), p. 25.
16. Lock, 'Deconstructing the Change', pp. 48–49.
17. Greer, *The Change*, pp. 24–25. Greer writes that the knowledge that women go through menopause at midlife is not new – Aristotle noted that women were unable to have children once they reached their fifth decade.
18. Ibid.
19. Lock, 'Deconstructing the Change', p. 46.
20. Gullette, 'Midlife Discourses', p. 27.
21. Lock, 'Deconstructing the Change', p. 51.
22. Ibid., p. 52.
23. Gullette, 'Midlife Discourses', p. 27.
24. Dorthe Nors, 'On the invisibility of middle-aged women', *Literary Hub*, 22 June 2016, para. 12: https://lithub.com/on-the-invisibility-of-middle-aged-women
25. 'Melissa McCarthy: "I was called grotesque by a reporter"', *Stuff*, 11

January 2019, paras 1–2: https://www.stuff.co.nz/entertainment/celebrities/109868412/melissa-mccarthy-i-was-called-grotesque-by-a-reporter

26. Chelsea Ritschel, 'Nike ad features woman with armpit hair', *Independent*, 25 April 2019, para. 7: www.independent.co.uk/life-style/nike-ad-instagram-armpit-hair-annahstasia-a8886901.html

27. Ariel Levy, 'Europe's Berlusconi Problem', *The New Yorker*, 27 October 2011, para. 3: www.newyorker.com/news/news-desk/europes-berlusconi-problem

28. Azmina Dhrodia, 'We tracked 25,688 abusive tweets sent to women MPs – half were directed at Diane Abbott', *New Statesman*, 5 September 2017, quote from image in para. 8: www.newstatesman.com/2017/09/we-tracked-25688-abusive-tweets-sent-women-mps-half-were-directed-diane-abbott

29. Ibid., para. 18.

30. Rebecca Mead, 'The Troll Slayer', *The New Yorker*, 25 August 2014, para. 2: www.newyorker.com/magazine/2014/09/01/troll-slayer

31. Family Violence Death Review Committee, *Family Violence Death Review Committee's Fifth Report Data: January 2009 to December 2015*, Health Quality and Safety Commission, 2017, p. 2: https://www.hqsc.govt.nz/assets/Uploads/FVDRC_media_summary_2017.pdf

32. Ibid.

33. Kate Maltby, 'Why is Elizabeth I, the most powerful woman in our history, always depicted as a grotesque?' *The Guardian*, 25 May 2015, para. 5: www.theguardian.com/commentisfree/2015/may/25/armada-documentary-ageing-woman-body-queen-elizabeth

34. Shweder, 'Preface', p. vii.

35. Shweder, 'Introduction', p. xi.

36. Shweder, 'Introduction', p. x.

37. Lock, 'Deconstructing the Change', p. 56.

38. Ibid., p. 46.

39. Ibid., p. 56.

40. Ibid., p. 61.

41. Ibid., p. 62.

42. Ibid.

43. Ibid., p. 63.

44. Ibid., p. 57.

45. Ibid., p. 58.

46. Ibid., p. 59.

47. Shore, 'Status Reversal', p. 102.

48. Ibid., p. 105.

49. Ibid., p. 133.

50. Taimalie Kiwi Tamasese, Tafaoimalo Loudeen Parsons and Charles Waldegrave, 'Pacific Perspectives on Ageing in New Zealand: Pacific-focused qualitative research, prepared for the New Zealand Longitudinal Study of Ageing (NZLSA)', The Family Centre, March 2014, p. 7: www.massey.ac.nz/massey/fms/Colleges/College%20of%20Humanities%20and%20Social%20Sciences/Psychology/HART/publications/reports/Pacific_Elders_NZLSA_2014.pdf

51. Ibid., pp. 10–11.

52. Shweder, 'Preface', p. vii.

53. Sohyun Chun, 'Blowing Away Convention: Enchi Fumiko, Tanabe Seiko and aging women in modern Japanese literature', PhD dissertation,

Washington University in St Louis, 2016, p. iv: https://openscholarship.wustl.edu/art_sci_etds/838

54. Shweder, 'Introduction', p. xvii.

55. '"Veil of silence" on Samoa's domestic violence', Radio New Zealand, September 12, 2018, paras 4–5: www.rnz.co.nz/international/pacific-news/366275/veil-of-silence-on-samoa-s-domestic-violence

56. Elizabeth Blair, 'Why are Old Women Often the Face of Evil in Fairy Tales and Folklore?', NPR, 28 October 2015, para. 2: www.npr.org/2015/10/28/450657717/why-are-old-women-often-the-face-of-evil-in-fairy-tales-and-folklore

57. Akiko Busch, 'The Invisibility of Older Women', *The Atlantic*, 28 February 2019: www.theatlantic.com/entertainment/archive/2019/02/akiko-busch-mrs-dalloway-shows-aging-has-benefits/583480/

58. C.E. Löckenhoff et al., 'Perceptions of Aging across 26 Cultures and their Culture-Level Associates', *Psychology and Aging*, vol. 24, no. 4, 2009: pp. 941–54, para. 2: www.ncbi.nlm.nih.gov/pmc/articles/PMC2933107

59. The study admits its own limitations: the sample was made up almost entirely of female university students, and participants from African and Middle Eastern countries were under-represented, as noted in the 'Discussion' section.

60. The students were asked about eight specific ageing perceptions: 'physical attractiveness', 'ability to do everyday tasks', 'ability to learn new information', 'general knowledge', 'wisdom', 'respect received from others', 'authority in the family', and 'life satisfaction'. See para. 11.

61. Löckenhoff et al., 'Perceptions of Aging', para. 25. The exceptions were 'Mainland China, India, Malaysia, Russia, and New Zealand, where participants reported neutral or slightly positive views'.

62. Ibid., Abstract.

63. Ibid., para. 43. This was summarised as: 'modernizing influences erode multi-generational family structures'.

64. Ibid., para. 42.

65. Ibid., para. 8.

66. Ibid., para. 34.

67. Ibid., para. 31.

68. Eleanor Gordon-Smith, '"I could make a little difference in the world but it seems like a lot of work. Is it worth trying?"', *The Guardian*, 18 November 2020, para. 7: www.theguardian.com/lifeandstyle/2020/nov/19/i-could-make-a-little-difference-in-the-world-but-it-seems-like-a-lot-of-work-is-it-worth-trying

Chapter Six: The crossing

1. Maggie Nelson, *The Argonauts* (Melbourne, Australia: Text Publishing, 2015), p. 81.

2. Murray Stein, '"Midway on our life's journey …": On psychological transformation at midlife', para. 2: www.murraystein.com/midway.shtml

3. Alok Vaid-Menon, *Beyond the Gender Binary* (New York: Penguin Workshop, 2020), p. 18.

4. Ibid., p. 19.

5. Ibid., p. 20.
6. Ibid.
7. Stein, 'Midway', para. 11.
8. Ibid.
9. Ibid., para. 12.
10. Bjørn Thomassen, *Liminality and the Modern: Living through the in-between* (Farnham, Surrey, and Burlington, VT: Ashgate, 2014), p. 1.
11. Victor Turner, *The Ritual Process: Structure and anti-structure* (New York: Routledge, 2017), p. 95.
12. Stein, 'Midway', para. 8.
13. Gary Kessler, *Fifty Key Thinkers on Religion* (London and New York: Routledge, 2012).
14. Ibid., p. 89.
15. Ibid., p. 90.
16. Julie Bien, 'A ritual to honor wisdom', *Jewish Journal*, 17 July 2013), para. 5: https://jewishjournal.com/ mobile_20111212/119295
17. Ibid., para. 4.
18. Sheetal Sharma, Edwin van Teijlingen, Vanora Hundley, Catherine Angell and Padam Simkhada, 'Dirty and 40 days in the wilderness: Eliciting childbirth and postnatal cultural practices and beliefs in Nepal', *BMC Pregnancy and Childbirth*, vol. 16, no. 1, July 2016: www.ncbi.nlm.nih.gov/pmc/articles/ PMC4933986/
19. Natalia Hailes, '4 Incredible Birthing Rituals From Different Cultures & Countries', *mindbodygreen*, 16 March 2020: www.mindbodygreen.com/ articles/birthing-rituals-of-different-countries
20. Germaine Greer, *The Change: Women, ageing and the menopause* (London: Hamish Hamilton, 1991), p. 49.
21. Harald Wydra, 'The Liminal Origins of Democracy', *International Political Anthropology*, vol. 2, no. 1, 2009, p. 103.
22. Turner, *The Ritual Process*, p. 96.
23. Lesley A. Northup, 'Pass-Aging: Women, Jiezhu, and life-cycle rituals', *Journal of Ritual Studies*, vol. 27, no. 2, 2013, p. 1: www.jstor.org/ stable/44368892
24. Ibid.
25. Ibid.
26. Greer, *The Change*, p. 46.
27. Suzanne Watson, interview by Karen Weese, 'Changing Channels: Stories of women reinventing themselves after 50', *Washington Post*, 9 June 2019, para. 4: www.washingtonpost.com/ graphics/2019/lifestyle/women-over-50/
28. Sandy Warshaw, interview by Laura Basset, 'Changing Channels', para. 2: www.washingtonpost.com/ graphics/2019/lifestyle/women-over-50/
29. Patricia Forehand, interview by Sonam Vashi, 'Changing Channels', para. 6: www.washingtonpost.com/ graphics/2019/lifestyle/women-over-50/
30. This quote is widely ascribed to Mary Ann Evans/George Eliot but I couldn't find any concrete evidence that she said or wrote these words.
31. Gullette, 'Midlife Discourses', p. 5.
32. Nelson, *The Argonauts*, p. 127.
33. *Diane*, directed by Kent Jones (United States: AgX, Sight Unseen Pictures, 2019).
34. Jeannette Catsoulis, '"Diane" Review: A vibrant tale of love, sisterhood and decline', *New York Times*, 28 March 2019, para. 6: www.nytimes. com/2019/03/28/movies/diane-review. html

Chapter Seven: The final call

1. David E. Stannard, review of Philippe Ariès, *Western Attitudes toward Death: From the Middle Ages to the present*, trans. Patricia M. Ranum, (Baltimore and London: the Johns Hopkins University Press, 1974), in *The American Historical Review*, vol. 80, no. 5, December 1975, p. 1297: doi: 10.1086/ahr/80.5.1297

2. Phillipe Ariès, *Western Attitudes toward Death: From the Middle Ages to the present*, trans. Patricia M. Ranum (Baltimore and London: the Johns Hopkins University Press, 1974), p. 105.

3. Stannard, review of Ariès, *Western Attitudes*, p. 1297.

4. Ibid.

5. Ariès, *Western Attitudes*, p. 87.

6. Ibid., p. 89.

7. Joanna B. Broad, Merryn Gott, Hongsoo Kim, Michal Boyd, He Chen and Martin J. Connolly, 'Where do people die? An international comparison of the percentage of deaths occurring in hospital and residential aged care settings in 45 populations, using published and available statistics', *International Journal of Public Health*, vol. 58, no. 2, April 2013, pp. 257–67, doi: 10.1007/s00038-012-0394-5

8. 'Cancer is New Zealand's biggest killer', *Stuff*, 8 May 2018: www.stuff.co.nz/business/industries/103546111/cancer-is-new-zealands-biggest-killer

9. J. Cohen, L Pivodic, G. Miccinesi, B.D. Onwuteaka-Philipsen, et al., 'International study of the place of death of people with cancer: A population-level comparison of 14 countries across 4 continents using death certificate data', *British Journal of Cancer*, vol. 113, no. 9, 2015, pp. 1397–404, doi: 10.1038/bjc.2015.312

10. Ariès, *Western Attitudes*, p. 88.

11. Atul Gawande, *Being Mortal: Medicine and what matters in the end* (London: Profile Books, 2014), p. 17.

12. Ariès, *Western Attitudes*, p. 99.

13. 'How Cremation Works', Auckland City Council: www.aucklandcouncil.govt.nz/cemeteries/cremation/Pages/how-cremation-works.aspx

14. Gawande, *Being Mortal*, pp. 76–77. While here Gawande is writing about nursing homes, he expresses similar sentiments about end-of-life care.

15. Ibid., p. 4.

16. Ibid., p. 5.

17. Ibid., pp. 5–6.

18. Carl Shuker, 'In the End', *Metro*, May 2015, pp. 94–97.

19. Ibid., p. 96.

20. Ibid., p. 97.

21. Gawande, *Being Mortal*, p. 158.

22. Emily Dickinson, 'Because I could not stop for Death – (479)', The Poetry Foundation: www.poetryfoundation.org/poems/47652/because-i-could-not-stop-for-death-479

23. Robert Hass, *Summer Snow* (United States: Ecco Press, 2020), p. 18.

24. Ibid., p. 21.

25. J.K. Rowling, *Harry Potter and the Philosopher's Stone*, illus. Jim Kay (London: Bloomsbury Publishing, 2015), p. 237.

26. Gawande, *Being Mortal*, p. 46.

27. Ariès, *Western Attitudes*, p. 106.

28. Darcey Steinke, *Flash Count Diary: A new story about the menopause* (Edinburgh: Canongate Books, 2019), p. 9.

29. Gawande, *Being Mortal*, p. 97.

30. Ibid., p. 95.

31. Anita Hannig, 'Talking About Death in America: An anthropologist's view', *Undark*, 19 October 2017: https://undark.org/2017/10/19/death-dying-america-anthropologist

32. Ibid., para. 4.

33. Larry Rosenberg, 'Death Awareness', *Tricycle Magazine*, vol. 7, no. 1, Fall 1997, para. 1: https://tricycle.org/magazine/death-awareness

34. Ibid., para. 4.

35. Ibid., para. 2.

36. Robert Pogue Harrison, *Juvenescence: A cultural history of our age* (Chicago and London: University of Chicago Press, 2014), p. 4.

Afterword

1. Rich Ferraro, 'Facebook introduces custom gender field to allow users to more accurately reflect who they are', Glaad, 13 February 2014, para. 1: www.glaad.org/blog/facebook-introduces-custom-gender-field-allow-users-more-accurately-reflect-who-they-are#:~:text=Facebook%20announced%20today%20that%20it,for%20the%20custom%20gender%20field

2. *Time*, vol. 183, no. 22, 9 June 2014.

3. Amanda Montañez, 'Beyond XX and XY: The extraordinary complexity of sex determination', *Scientific American*, vol. 317, no. 3, September 2017, pp. 50–51, doi: 10.1038/scientificamerican0917-50

4. Reed Blaylock, 'For linguists, it was the decade of the pronoun', *The Conversation*, 8 January 2020: https://theconversation.com/for-linguists-it-was-the-decade-of-the-pronoun-128606

5. Jacob Tobia, 'Everything You Ever Wanted to Know About Gender-Neutral Pronouns', *Time*, 12 May 2016, para. 1: https://time.com/4327915/gender-neutral-pronouns

6. Maggie Nelson, *The Argonauts* (Melbourne, Australia: Text Publishing, 2015), p. 65.

KA HAEA TE ATA is the first line of a Kāi Tahu karakia that welcomes the new day.

Published by Otago University Press
Te Whare Tā o Te Wānanga o Ōtākou
533 Castle Street
Dunedin, New Zealand
university.press@otago.ac.nz
www.otago.ac.nz/press

First published 2022
Text copyright © Sarah Jane Barnett

ISBN 978-1-99004836-4

Published with the assistance of Creative New Zealand

Editor: Anna Hodge
Design and layout: Fiona Moffat
Cover image: Henrietta Harris, *Fixed It XVI*, 2016. Oil on linen, 750 x 600mm.
Private collection, New Zealand. Courtesy of the artist and Melanie Roger Gallery.

Printed in Aotearoa New Zealand by Ligare.